In Praise of Forgiveness

To Luciana Sica,
to her strength

Massimo Recalcati

In Praise of Forgiveness

Translated by Alice Kilgarriff

polity

First published in Italian as *Non è più come prima*. Copyright © 2014, Raffaello Cortina Editore. All rights reserved. Published by arrangement with The Italian Literary Agency.
This English edition (c) Polity Press, 2020

Excerpts from REMEMBRANCE OF THINGS PAST, VOLUME III: THE CAPTIVE, THE FUGITIVE, THE PAST RECAPTURED by Marcel Proust, translated by C. K. Scott Moncrieff and Terence Kilmartin, and by Andreas Mayor, translation copyright © 1981 by Penguin Random House LLC and Chatto & Windus. Used by permission of Random House, an imprint and division of Penguin Random House LLC. All rights reserved.

Polity Press
65 Bridge Street
Cambridge CB2 1UR, UK

Polity Press
101 Station Landing
Suite 300
Medford, MA 02155, USA

ISBN-13: 978-1-5095-3489-0
ISBN-13: 978-1-5095-3490-6 (pb)

A catalogue record for this book is available from the British Library.

Library of Congress Cataloging-in-Publication Data

Names: Recalcati, Massimo, author. | Kilgarriff, Alice, translator.
Title: In praise of forgiveness / Massimo Recalcati ; translated by Alice Kilgarriff.
Other titles: Non è più come prima. English
Description: English edition. | Cambridge, UK ; Medford, MA, USA : Polity Press, 2020. | Summary: "An original reflection on betrayal and forgiveness in modern relationships"-- Provided by publisher.
Identifiers: LCCN 2019038645 (print) | LCCN 2019038646 (ebook) | ISBN 9781509534890 (hardback) | ISBN 9781509534906 (paperback) | ISBN 9781509534913 (epub)
Subjects: LCSH: Forgiveness. | Interpersonal relations.
Classification: LCC BF637.F67 R43 2020 (print) | LCC BF637.F67 (ebook) | DDC 158.2--dc23
LC record available at https://lccn.loc.gov/2019038645
LC ebook record available at https://lccn.loc.gov/2019038646
A catalogue record for this book is available from the British Library.

Typeset in 12 on 15 pt Fournier MT by
Servis Filmsetting Ltd, Stockport, Cheshire
Printed and bound in Great Britain by TJ International Limited

The publisher has used its best endeavours to ensure that the URLs for external websites referred to in this book are correct and active at the time of going to press. However, the publisher has no responsibility for the websites and can make no guarantee that a site will remain live or that the content is or will remain appropriate.

Every effort has been made to trace all copyright holders, but if any have been overlooked the publisher will be pleased to include any necessary credits in any subsequent reprint or edition.

For further information on Polity, visit our website: politybooks.com

Contents

Acknowledgements

I would like to thank my friend and editor Raffaello Cortina for having believed in me over these last few years, and Maria Egidi with whom I share a great deal of my working life and who, over ten years of working together, has supported me with patience, affection and happiness. Federica Manzon and Lucrezia Lerro for their friendship and for having read and commented upon the narrative parts of the book, giving me invaluable advice. My thanks also to Mauro Grimoldi for having listened to me discuss this book since its conception during our morning runs through Parco Sempione and elsewhere. Last but not least, Enzo Bianchi for his silent presence in me.

The most precious gift that marriage gave me was the constant impact of something very close and intimate, yet all the time unmistakably other, resistant – in a word, real.

C. S. Lewis, *A Grief Observed*

Introduction

The psychoanalyst hears the woes that accompany love lives on a daily basis: emotional isolation, sexual inhibitions and symptoms, the compulsive quest for relationships that fail to satisfy, the ensuing disappointment, the initial ecstasy of falling in love, infidelity, boredom, jealousy, a decline in desire, separation, abuse, the inability to love, the difficulty of finding the right man or woman. And yet today's trials and tribulations of love seem to be different from those of the past. Sexual freedom and female emancipation, to cite just two of the most relevant phenomena of the last few decades, have upset a certain stereotype of amorous suffering. The desperate Platonism of those who, faced with a frustrating reality, cultivate their inhibited passions in secret has given way to a diffuse disinhibition and the multiplication of sexual and loving experiences in an entirely liberated way. Everything seems to be consumed far more quickly, without moral censure or obstacles. Criticism of any institutionalization of bonds between the sexes seems to have become the politically correct norm, whilst the collective cult of a love without ties is an illusion that has generated nothing more than will-o'-the-wisps. The invocation of absolute freedom and the intolerance shown to any form of bond that implies responsibility have led to a new master. We no longer have the master who carries the stick of prohibition, but one who demands an enjoyment that is always New and that consequently experiences a long-term relationship as a gas chamber killing off the mysterious fascination of desire. One father dies and another takes his place: the time of mourning is maniacally rejected as unnecessarily sad and extravagant. Rather than painfully processing the loss of a beloved object, it is preferable to replace it as quickly as possible, conforming to the dominant logic that governs the capitalist discourse: if an object no longer works, you mustn't feel nostalgic about it! Exchange it for an upgraded model!

At a time in which everything seems to respond to the perverse siren song of the New, this book aims to be a song dedicated to love that resists and that persists in its vindication of the bond with what does not pass, with what is able to stand the test of time, with what cannot be consumed. It does not deal with those infatuations that burn out without a trace in just one night. It delves into that love that lasts a lifetime, that leaves its mark, that does not want to die, that disproves Freud's cynical belief that love and desire are destined to lie apart because the existence of one (love) necessarily excludes that of the other (sexual desire).[1] It looks at that love in which desire grows and does not fade with the passing of time because with it the horizons of the lovers' bodies, and the world itself, are erotically expanded. That love in which the ecstasy of the encounter insists on repeating itself, on wanting the other again, on staying faithful to itself, in which the headiness is not diluted but gives meaning to time, rendering it eternal. This is a love animated by what the poet Paul Éluard, once cited by Jacques Lacan, defines 'le dur désir du durer' ['the firm desire to endure'].[2]

This book asks what happens to these bonds when one person cheats on the other, when one falls short of the promise made, living another emotional experience mired in secret and deceit. What happens to those loving relationships crushed by the trauma of betrayal and abandonment? What happens when the person who has cheated then asks for forgiveness? What if they ask to be loved once more, despite having decreed that it was not like it used to be, and want everything to go back to how it was before? Is forgiveness truly possible in these cases? Or must we limit ourselves to repeating the Freudian sentence according to which all love is a narcissistic dream, a promise that does not exist, a love that never lasts 'forever', there being no love for the Other that is not love for ourselves? Must we spit on love, making fun of lovers in their efforts to make love last?

Freud's analysis, developed in his 'Contributions to the Psychology of Love',[3] is only interested in describing the neurotic version of love. His theory on the gulf between sexual desire and love that leads human beings to split the object of their erotic enjoyment from that of their love has often been misunderstood, as if reconciling the level of the body's sexual enjoyment with that of love as a gift of oneself to the Other were a structural impossibility. We must be clear: if psychoanalytic treatment deals with this (neurotic) split between sexual enjoyment and loving tenderness towards the Other, this does not mean that such a split is the structural cipher of love. What is the point of psychoanalysis if not precisely to make bonds possible that allow loving desire towards the Other to converge with the erotic enjoyment of the body? Isn't this one of the most relevant issues at stake? We know it from experience: love in which loving desire is not in any way split from sexual enjoyment but grows exponentially alongside erotic passion for the body of the Other does exist. This was what led Lacan to define love as *the only* possibility of allowing desire to converge with enjoyment without any neurotic disassociation.[4]

This book does not delve into the pathology of the split between desire and enjoyment, but examines an aspect of love that is as important as it is strangely sidelined by psychoanalysis: forgiveness. It treats forgiveness as one of the most noble and difficult tests awaiting lovers.

The work of forgiveness is always preceded by the trauma of betrayal and abandonment. The loved object vanishes, it is transfigured, it moves away. We know that all trauma, in a single seismic movement, affects the very meaning of the world and our existence in it. It is not just the loved object that is missing, but the very order of the world smashed to pieces by that loss, becoming unrecognizable and descending into pure non-sense.

How can the ashes of this retreat by the other be inhabited without destroying everything? How is it possible to resist betraying the promise? Much like the work of mourning, the work of forgiveness requires extra time in order to be carried out. Sometimes this hits a wall that can be impossible to overcome, that of loss of trust in the word of the Other. Forgiveness can then become impossible precisely because of love. This is one of the theories posited in this book: the failure of forgiveness is no less important than a successful work of forgiveness. Various patients talk about an irreversible collapse of their trust in the Other that can never be fixed. Who can blame them? In these cases too, the subject finds themselves facing the wall of impossibility: they cannot forgive, they cannot forgive the wound left by the deceit because to forgive would mean to forget, to not want to know, to pretend nothing had happened, to not face up to all the consequences that the traumatic truth of betrayal and abandonment have unleashed. At other times, the work of forgiveness challenges the unforgivable and saves love by resisting the temptation of revenge. This is its mysterious joy: the one that allows for a brand-new beginning, an absolute new beginning.

No love, not even that which exists within the promise to last 'forever', is safe from the risk of ending, because every human love always implies absolute exposure to the Other, and never excludes the possibility of its retraction and disappearance. In all of those situations in which the traumatic impact of betrayal has brought love to its knees, is it truly possible that the work of forgiveness can restore life to that which seemed to be irremediably dead? This is the real question at the heart of this book.

The Ideology of the New

The Contemporary Degradation of Love Lives

Love is a trap, a hoax, an illusion destined to melt like snow in the sunshine, the result of a sleep of reason, a deception, a trick played on us by our neuroendocrine system. Every love dies a death sooner or later, revealing its artificial nature. Time corrodes passion, proclaiming its end, demoting it to an administration of goods and services. After the initial ecstatic upheaval provoked by the influx of dopamine into certain parts of the brain, every loving bond flattens into a routine lacking in desire. Time inevitably kills the enthusiasm that surrounds the emotion of that first encounter. Without the stimulation offered by the New, every love ends up in the quicksand of an alienating intimacy, deprived of eroticism. For entire generations, the white vest worn by the head of the family was, according to Adorno, the symbol of this decline of desire into the charade of family life.[1] This traditional version of the alienation of family ties is probably best represented today with the image of a couple lying on a sofa watching television, or a man and a woman who, rather than conversing or sharing enthusiasm for their own projects,

6

immerse themselves autistically in the closed-off worlds of their own iPhones.

In modern life, erotic desire appears to be rigidly alternative to the family bond. The existence of this bond causes it to fade or vanish, because it is constructed on the very interdiction of that desire. There is no escaping this. Either desire or family: this seems to be the refrain of contemporary hyper-hedonism. What about psychoanalysis? Hasn't it also contributed to the emergence of this truth? Has its own doctrine not demonstrated how the split between love and sexual desire has accompanied human life from its very first loving relationships? Is this not the split referred to by Freud when he theorizes about the most common degradation of loving relationships? The mother's body as the locus of the child's first intense loving experiences is forbidden to desire. This irreconcilability between love and sexual desire leads men to transform their partners into mothers and search for erotic passion in women outside the family, fantasizing about these women offering sex without love. This is the classic disjuncture between the loved woman, mother of his children and life partner, and the woman-whore with whom he can live out all kinds of erotic passions with great intensity. It is the Freudian disjuncture between the loving flow of tenderness and that of sexual desire.[2] It is as if desire's condition of vitality were nothing more than the perverse staging of the Law's transgression. If the Father's prohibition strikes the woman-mother, this feeds the subject's urge to search for the object of desire beyond the jurisdiction of the family as the locus of prohibited objects. It is from this original prohibition that the split between the flow of tenderness and that of sexual desire takes shape, drawn in the subject's life like two parallel lines that, despite being stretched out infinitely, will never meet: the loved woman can never coincide with the woman of desire.

Freud had perhaps failed to predict that this common degradation of a love life is no longer today the exclusive burden of the male sex, but also extends into the female world. Antonia tells me during her analysis about how her emotional life is entirely split from a marital bond that has become boring and deprived of enthusiasm, and a relationship with a colleague that pushes her to have sexual encounters that border on abuse. The deep esteem in which she holds her husband is irreversibly detached from desire and is equally matched by the contempt for her lover, which seems paradoxically to feed it. Antonia is clearly split: the tenderness of her husband is as impossible to give up as the transgressive erotic charge that she finds in the other man. In this way, her life appears to be afflicted by the very split pinpointed by Freud as the paradigm of degradation in the male love life. The hard-earned sexual freedom of women thus risks following the missteps taken by the male neuroses: experiencing one's partner as a limit, aspiring to a bond that goes beyond the family unit as the only experience of practising one's own sexual desire in a vital and non-repetitive way.

But there are many variations on the Freudian framework. For example, one man in analysis told me of his need to cheat on his wife, whom he declared he loved deeply. In this case, the libidinal and erotic value of this couple's sex life had remained intact after many years of marriage. At play here was not, then, the classic disarticulation of emotional life and erotic passion, of the flow of tenderness and that of sexual desire. Rather, it appeared evident that the condition that had preserved the sexual understanding and family love in this couple was the very reason this man had always cheated on his wife. In this way, he would repeatedly make her a lost object and, therefore, extremely desirable. He required the existence of a lover in order to de-complete his wife, rendering her lacking and therefore activating her once more as a subject of desire emancipated from the family routine.[3]

Resignation or Dopamine?

Couples separate, marriages fail, the length of bonds is shortened: this is a fact. The birth of a child often coincides in particular with a crisis in the bond on both sides. The man has trouble locating the woman with whom he fell in love in the woman who has become a mother, and the woman, identifying the man as the father of her family, remains sexually unsatisfied and searches for the object capable of resuscitating her erotic desire in an other.[4] Psychoanalytic practice can offer infinite examples of this tendency. But its basis lies in the falsehood that today endorses the equivalence between the New and happiness. This lie forces us to live in desperate search of the New with the (false) supposition that in the New we will find full self-realization. The ridiculing of loving pathos towards the absolute, the promise of lovers that it will be 'forever', not only comes from cynical disenchantment, but also and most significantly from the social imperative of the New and its explosive combination with a reductively machine-like version of the human being that scientific research seems to corroborate. An eloquent example of this is given by the great biologist and neuroscientist Robin Dunbar when he reminds us, rapidly cooling the boiling spirits of naïve lovers who experience a kiss with romantic abandon, that the kiss is probably, more than anything else, a test of the health and genetics of future partners. That it concerns health is obvious because poor health often results in bad breath and an acidic taste in the mouth, two things that are easily ascertained when we kiss.[5]

The point is that in our time the difficulty of uniting sexual enjoyment with love, which as we have seen was considered by Freud to be the most common neurosis in any love life, has become emblematic of a truth that seems undeniable: desire is destined to die if its object is not constantly renewed, if we do not change partner, if it is closed for too long in the restrictive chamber of the same bond. The proliferation of divorce and separations seems to support this truth beyond any doubt. It is beyond discussion. In a long-term conjugal bond, or even when simply living together, the erotic urge of desire is destined at the very least to grow numb, if not to disappear altogether. The materialistic cynicism of modern hyper-hedonism seems to find support in the most advanced scientific research. Falling in love is much like doping, its effects destined to fade in the space of a few months (between three and eighteen, apparently). In a loving encounter, the areas of the brain that deal with judgement and critical analysis are clouded by a rise in dopamine, the hormone that activates our most irrational and euphoric urges. But this cloud is time-limited and must either evolve into a state of monogamous calm, as promoted by the activation of oxytocin receptors, or feverishly revive itself through a new encounter.[6]

Faced with this cynical, scientific demolition of love, it seems there are two remaining options: to accept the inevitable corruption of the bond and regularly change partners in order to revitalize one's own love life (a change that can also lead to a parallel love life being maintained, as is the case with affairs), or to resign oneself to a life without desire, to the monotony of the family charade, guaranteeing oneself monogamous emotional security as a counterpart to the acceptance of the mortal desiccation of desire.

But are these really the only paths we can follow? Can psychoanalysis accept that the loving discourse be reduced to the vacuous metonymy of desire or the disenchanted resignation to the boredom provided by the reality principle? Does this not fall short of its critical mission, that of refusing any conformist accommodation of desire?

We must be clear that our times are not the same as those experienced by Freud. Back then, psychoanalysis had made a significant critical contribution to the deconstruction of the romantic Ideal of love, demonstrating how this Ideal was often a cover for the obscene, unspeakable real of the drive. It was therefore used to unmake love as an artificial Ideal that ended up imposing a straitjacket on the unconscious power of desire. The suspicions of the psychoanalyst revealed how greed and affirmation of the Ego went hand in hand with all altruistic sentiment, like a heavy shadow, including that of love. This is a thesis that we find not only in Freud but in the majority of reflections, even the most recent, made by psychoanalysts on the subject of love. Love is a trick, the effect of a temporary blindness that leads us to mistake the other for our ideal Ego.[7] The truth is that the urge of the drive reduces the value of the object to a mere instrument of its own demand for satisfaction. What counts is the satisfaction of the drive, to which the particular existence of the object is entirely indifferent. This is one of Freud's theories that demonstrates the entirely secondary ('variable') character of the beloved object: the drive demands the satisfaction of the One, who is not at all interested in the fate of the Other.[8]

Narcissistic Love

The heretical moment foretold by psychoanalysis contains within it a rightful demand: to demonstrate the extent to which narcissistic love is an illusion that does not feed the bond with the Other, but that reinforces the Ego's passionate, one-way devotion to itself. When I say 'I love you', I am also saying 'I love myself through you.' Freud is clear on this point: when I choose to love the Other, I choose to love the person who represents the ideal image of my Ego. Love can have many sides and one of these is without doubt that of a scam, of blindness, of suggestion, of hypnosis, of narcissistically falling in love.[9]

Today, this act of unmasking the loving Ideal has ended up fatally colluding with the hyper-hedonistic cynicism of the capitalist discourse. Psychoanalysis has unwittingly served the new master – the capitalist discourse – which decrees love to be an illusion, whilst insisting that what counts in life is the acquisition of the highest possible quota of enjoyment. It is also for this reason that the time has come for psychoanalysis to say something more on love. If this disenchantment has come from the dominant ideology that dismisses everything beyond the closed horizon of the Ego as naïve belief and pure misrecognition, then psychoanalysis needs to rediscover the role it plays in sustaining critical social theory, recovering the dimension of love as absolute exposure, as an irreducible and unique point of resistance in the face of the cynical and narcissistic bent that feeds the capitalist discourse. This means revaluating psychoanalysis, seeing it as a possible *discourse on love* that cannot be absorbed by either the libertine worship of desire without ties or the bourgeois resignation to lifeless routine, rather than solely as a force that deconstructs the loving Ideal. Is it not up to psychoanalysis, today more than ever, to endorse once more the dimension of love in its absolute risk? Should psychoanalysis itself not wager the existence of a new love, a 'new love' capable, as Lacan would have said, of making desire (as a demand for love that makes the loved one unique and irreplaceable) and enjoyment (as the urge of an erotic body of drive) converge with love rather than dissociate from it?

Two Lies for Our Time

Our time is built upon two fundamental lies about the nature of human beings. The first sees them as independent, free, autonomous, free from symbolic debts to the Other from which they hail. This is the narcissistic lie that feeds the individualistic cult of one's own image and that, in turn, lays the basis for the fantasy of liberty and self-generation, the ideal of making a name for oneself without passing through the Other.

The second lie exalts the New as the guiding principle in the life of desire. This lie maintains that goodness, salvation and satisfaction reside in what we do not yet possess: in the new object, the new partner, the new sensation. From this comes a purely nihilistic version of desire, which works to breathlessly pursue that which, in reality, is destined to always be lacking.[10]

These two great lies of our time are bound together, reinforcing one another. Making a name for oneself without passing through the Other – misrecognizing the symbolic debt that ties us to it – feeds a purely perverse version of freedom as being able to do exactly as we please. The crazed racing of desire between one object and the next seems to therefore take on the traits of a genuinely collective hallucination. Desire is pulled like a magnet towards the new object, the new sensation, the new encounter, the new love. Goodness is never found in what we have but always deferred, to be found in that which we do not yet possess. And it is precisely here that the machine of the capitalist discourse finds the principle of its own function: not to meet needs but to transform them into pseudo-desires that are impossible to satisfy and that, precisely because of this impossibility, appear to be perennially enticed by the siren song of the New Object. This is the hyper-modern version of the capitalist machine that carries with it the absence of care for what we have and the compulsive urge to reach that which we lack, reducing lack to a void that yearns mindlessly to be filled, though this is, in reality, always deferred.[11] Total satisfaction is postponed in a beyond that reveals itself to be inaccessible. So boredom sets in even more quickly, living off relationships like a parasite, feeding the unsatisfied urge towards that which we do not have. This framework obviously also has an impact on loving bonds, with devastating and, paradoxically, illusionistic consequences. Isn't this perhaps the radical disenchantment that, as we have seen, reduces the kiss to hygienic safeguarding, and falling in love to an onslaught of dopamine destined to rapidly run out, before creating a new form of enchantment? The hypnotic suggestion provoked by the New turns love that lasts, love that wants to be forever, into nothing more than a meaningless word, or worse, an advertising slogan. Shouldn't we then think today that the great illusion is no longer that of an everlasting love, but the destruction of love as an effect of the exaltation of a freedom made of nothingness? And if this were the case, would love that refuses to retreat when faced with commitment, at risk of absolute exposure, not be a unique point of resistance to its cynical liquidation as promoted by modern cynicism?

The New Libertine Ideology

The libertine regime is sustained by the enchantment of the New, which dissolves any representation of the eternal, considering it a childish product of the human imagination. It aims to render any lasting encounter impossible. It wants to unmask fidelity to the Same as if it were a lie. The desire that wants to be entirely free rejects any idea of fidelity and constancy in the name of a permanent spontaneity. The capitalist discourse experiences every kind of bond as an obstacle to its unquestioned affirmation. In this sense, humans are reduced to nothing more than goods in an even more radical way than that described by Marx. Bonds seem to be unable to hold in the face of a freedom that wants to be absolute, rejecting any experience of the limit. The generalized hyperactivity fed by the capitalist discourse deludes us, causing us to believe that there are no second chances, that what counts in this is not even the accumulation of enjoyment, as the ascetic-Weberian version of capitalism would have it, but its multiplication.[12] For this reason, every bond becomes a limit, a point of resistance to the crazed motion of the capitalist discourse's unchecked machine. Everything is rendered volatile in a purely nihilistic regime of desire, in which, as Lacan wrote, it is not so much the subject that confuses its prey with its shadow, as if there were some kind of visual defect, but the subject itself that is *prey to the shadow*.[13]

This maniacal acceleration of time makes the loving promise that it be 'everlasting' laughable, naïve, even stupidly superstitious. Bonds are shredded by the logic of the New, which, in increasingly short time frames, makes the Same a left-over from the past that must be replaced as quickly as possible. The simple epidemiology of relationships demonstrates this: human beings are struggling more and more to remain in one bond for any length of time. Separations abound, married or long-term couples leave each other with increasing frequency in order to create new bonds or to live out their own freedom in a more carefree manner. It is a sign of the times. As Bauman rightly asserted, ours is an age of liquid loves.[14] This is the age of libertinism as an unprecedented duty of the Super-Ego. In the place of the symbolic pact that binds two lovers, of which the marriage bonds are the greatest symbol, a disenchanted cynicism establishes itself, one that views every bond as time-limited, destined to spoil and be exchanged for a new one. We search for the New to break the routine, the boredom of the familiar, the anonymous ordinariness of our lives. We search for the spice of falling in love in order to add flavour to our desire-less lives. The growing refusal of the symbolic pact of marriage, to which living together is increasingly preferred, is a telling sign. Couples unite and fall apart without passing through the Other, without pondering the symbolic value of the pact. At play here is a purely pubescent view of desire that wants to avoid any assumption of responsibility. The presence of the symbolic pact with the Other would kill the freedom and vitality of desire. The disarming consequence of this new libertine ideology is the decline of the loving bond into little more than the stuff of gossip about summer love affairs. The ideological distortion of love is evident and it gives rise to a refrain that never changes: *the intensity of loving passion stands in relentless opposition to the length of the relationship*. The time spent together would fatally extinguish the flame of desire, which would supposedly always require the storm of emotion that is by its very nature profoundly anti-institutional. The merry-go-round of bonds makes a mockery of the expectation of eternity contained within the promise made by lovers. However, psychoanalytic practice is stating the obvious when it finds that the compulsive search for the New is not in any way an expression of freedom, but a new slavery, the result of an ideological social injunction ('Enjoy!') to which the subject must radically submit.

Love as Resistance to the Libertine Worship of the New

The demand accompanying every real love, notably that it be everlasting, resists the nihilistic tendencies of our time. It upholds, in an old-fashioned way, the assertion that the loving bond is not destined to dissolve over time, but that in that bond time appears as a sudden and powerful figure of the eternal.[15] It does not follow the current trend, it does not deride the promises made by lovers, and it does not want to reiterate the relativity of every loving bond in a politically correct way. Here we have love as an erotic force, a manifestation of Eros, the force of the bond according to Freud, a force that resists time and that introduces time to the single experience of the absolute conceded to human beings: that of the loving bond as a bond with a unique Other, an Other that is irreplaceable, impossible to reproduce. Love that lasts reveals the entirely illusory nature of the Super-Ego's injunction of the New, demonstrating to us how the most authentic experience of the New can only take place within the Same. The psychoanalyst sees this every day: the New as an (illusory) cure for the bored repetition of the Same always leads life back to the same lack of satisfaction. This is what patients caught in the spiral of continually changing partners complain about. Each time they describe the new love as ideal, full of promise, different and unique, each time in just a short, if not incredibly short time, they find it to be disappointing, inadequate and sadly identical to all the others.

Love that lasts *resists* the corrosive urge of enjoyment as an end in itself and refuses the illusion that happiness lies in the New, in what we do not possess. Thus, love is the New which, rather than attacking *the* bond, transforms itself *into* a bond. It does not experience joy just for a moment, but obstinately demands its infinite repetition, because it is only through repetition that it can show the true face, the only credible face of the New. According to Heidegger, the force of the loving bond therefore becomes similar to that of a work of art: *it allows a refounding of the openness to the world*.[16] This is why lovers live in a world that is no longer the same one as before, that of the One on their own, because this world is lived in a brand new way as a Two. It is, therefore, a new opening onto the world, a world viewed not from the point of view of one alone, but of the Two.[17] It is only this new perspective that allows us to experience the New in the Same, as happens *every* time the spring wind blows into Milan exposing the blue peaks of the Alps *every* year at the end of *every* winter. It is the Same wind each time every year, and each time every year it is new. It is the same surprise that accompanies the Two in seeing mushrooms spring up on forest floors, or observing the portulaca flowers on the terrace of the house by the sea resist the force of the wind.[18] *Each* time the Same and *each* time entirely New. Is this not the Same enchantment that accompanies a life spent together in lasting love, in love that resists the empty siren song of the New, even in its most modest ordinariness? Is it not her that I always love as Other in being herself? Is the same day not a New one in light of love? Is it not what I have that, thanks to love, becomes New each time? Is it not love that reveals the repetition of everyday things to be pure poetry, like the strength of the image that does not pass, that is suspended and sits outside of time? The Morandi-esque attention to things in the world that is found in the most recent poetry by Francesco Scarabicchi is one of the highest and most intense glorifications of the shared time of things bending towards the eternal.[19] This is why when Lacan dedicated one of his most intense and original Seminars to the subject of love he decided to call it *Encore*, again, again, *encore*.[20] 'Again' is, in essence, the basic form taken by the demand for love. Again, again, the Same again, again like today, again like now, once more, again. To want the Same again, the Same that is never enough, that you want to drink because it quenches thirst and, at the same time, feeds a new thirst that is never quenched, but that grows precisely as you try to quench it without every truly managing. It is only in the gift of life that there is a growth of the self, a strengthening and expansion of life that is able to live the absolute exposure to the desire of the Other. This is one of the decisive theses put forward by Saint Augustine: love is not *cupiditas* [lust, greed], it is not the greedy consumption of the Other, but the gift of oneself that causes those who give it to grow.[21] Is this not deep down the strange substance from which love is made? A substance that the more it is given, the more it concedes, the more it is consumed, the more it enriches, grows and expands. This is why the young Hegel wanted to carve all of the mystery and power of love into the words Shakespeare's Juliet says to her Romeo: 'The more I give to thee, the more I have.'[22]

Encounter and Destiny

Love as Oedipal Repetition

The first characteristic of love, as argued by Freud, is that of repetition, which causes the choice of the object to be led by the unconscious fantasy: the love for a man or a woman is a copy of infantile Oedipal love for the father or mother. Psychoanalytic treatment is able each time to locate the starting point of this repetition, which intervenes to unconsciously alter the bonds of love. This is the case, for example, with Gaia, a woman in her forties tormented by consistently unhappy relationships with men. When she comes to see me, she formulates her request for analysis in this way: 'I've come to see you to know why I always choose men who turn out to be torturers.' Having had a very authoritarian father, she had constructed the idea that the men she chose were duplicates of him. Soon, however, her analysis led her to confront another truth. Rather than being torturers, the men she chose all had the habit of making her feel 'brilliant', making her 'very happy' but then, almost immediately after, making her feel 'terrible', making her 'very unhappy', thus forcing her to live an impetuous rollercoaster of emotions. Gaia discovered that this 'up and down' was a typical trait of her relationship with her mother, who would fill her with praise and approval of all kinds, making her happy, but then for no apparent reason would denigrate her, dropping her like an 'empty sack'.

In Adele's case, the repetition occurred in a different way. This woman had been cheated on by her partner and the father of her children, who had had an affair with her brother's wife. Adele not only had to bear the traumatic wound of betrayal, but also the fact that her man had altered all internal relationships with her family, to which she was very close. Analysis would reveal to her that she had bound herself to this man precisely because of that character trait – 'coldness' – that she said she hated. This coldness was associated with that of her beloved father, too dedicated to his own professional life and other women to dedicate himself to loving her mother and his family. Her Oedipus had fixed her onto this love for the father as someone who lives in a state of total emotional independence, impossible to reach, 'cold'. And all of this was repeated with the betrayal, and only after several years of analysis would she be able to recognize her role in having skilfully and unconsciously orchestrated it.

In Daniela's case too, the choice of the object of love seems to be Oedipally fixed. She turns to the analyst because she cannot bear her partner's violence, bemoaning his duplicity. She knows he is as beastly and insensitive as he is sweet and loving. The point of her fantasmatic fixation dates back to her childhood, when she discovered her father's secret, overhearing a number of telephone calls between him and his lover.

Thus, she encountered the fundamental duplicity of her Other: the hard-working family man who had been cultivating a clandestine relationship with a fancy woman for years. Daniela was unable to reconcile these two faces of the paternal Other, just as she was unable to leave her boyfriend. What kept her there was the very duplicity she bemoaned: he made her feel incredibly loved and then immediately after, he humiliated her. The duplicity of the Oedipal father affected her in this way through the unconscious grip of repetition.

Falling in Love with Ourselves

Freud's second theory on human love is that it is structurally narcissistic. Its insurmountable foundation is love for oneself. The loved one always appears as a form of imaginary alienation of the subject's I. I love in the other that which I would like to be and am not, in him I love my unattainable Ideal. Freud models the bond of love on the physical schema of communicating vases: the loved object captures the libidinal investment of the subject, emptying it. The libido of the One is poured into the recipient of the Other and the more the object is loved, and is narcissistically overvalued – 'overestimated' – the more the subject is enslaved. The loved object thus occupies the post of an idol to whom the subject dedicates itself fully, in a suggestive relationship of total dependency and critical blindness. The real defects of the loved one disappear, mysteriously sublimated in an exultant idealization that dresses them in the finest, most majestic clothes. It happens, then, that the more the Other is enriched, the more the subject is impoverished. The I of the one who loves collapses before the power of the loved object that has vampirically fed on their libido. It should not be any surprise therefore that this schema is essentially the same as the one proposed by Feuerbach in his reading of religious aliena-tion.[1] The human being attributes traits from their own being to God, entertaining a purely regressive relationship with it, no longer able to recognize those traits as their own. Religious alienation, much like that in a loving relationship, would there-fore be the human being losing their own essence. Blindness, overestimation, impoverishment, infatuation, idealization: all words with which Freud defines the narcissistic phenomenon of falling in love.[2]

Today this purely imaginary version of love ends up collud-ing with the capitalist discourse, which demonstrates how the only law the drive obeys is that of the continuous replacement of the object, its compulsive and predatory consumption. At its core is not absolute exposure to the desire of the Other but the triumph of the Object, the chaotic multiplication of partial objects, as occurs in pornography void of any eroticism, in which we are not even offered the image of the erotic body in its aesthetic extension, because bodies are reduced to holes, ori-fices, tools, devices, detached objects (vaginas, anuses, mouths, hands, eyes, feet, buttocks, breasts, and so on) that join together in a way that is detached from the (phallic) image of the body, all mechanically manifesting themselves in the most complete anonymity. This is the perverse faith of the existence of the Object that, according to Pasolini, surpasses the faith in the

Other of love, consuming the passage without return from the monotheism of the old God to the objectal polytheism of the capitalist discourse.[3]

The Scream of Life

If we want to say something new about love, something on love that goes beyond repetition and narcissism, we must leave Freud and join Lacan. It is the French psychoanalyst's aim to go beyond Freudian reductionism whilst maintaining love as distinct from every ideal of harmony, concord or conciliation of the One with the Other. He, like me, is not happy to reduce love to passion for the I of oneself. He wants to try to emancipate love from its Oedipal (or pre-Oedipal) repetition and the imaginary specularity that confuses the I with the Other and vice versa.

The first step Lacan takes past Freud demonstrates how there is no possibility for human life without the presence of the Other. The child initially recognizes its own body as a continuous source of sensations that are not integrated with one another but instead generate the experience of feeling oneself dominated by one's own body, which is experienced as a stranger. The body does not appear as an order, but as a disorder, a chaos without meaning, an excess that bursts through the boundaries of the organism. This is what Lacan refers to with the figure of the 'fragmented body' (*corps morcelé*) that precedes that unifying experience of the mirror, which, by allowing the subject to have a specular representation that assembles the various parts of the body, reclaims the chaos that runs through it.[4] With the German term *Hilflosigkeit* he defined the human condition as dominated from the outset by a lack of governance, by a dispossession, a loss of control. The etymology of this word unites the term *Hilf*, meaning help, with *los* – loss. It refers to the original experience of a loss of help, of feeling oneself fall, without support, abandoned by the Other. In Italian this term is canonically translated with the terms 'defencelessness', 'dereliction' or 'impotence'. In *Seminar X* Lacan proposes it should be translated with the more lyrical and more effective expression 'abandonment', absolute abandonment.[5]

Think of the simple experience of a fever for a child in its first weeks of life. Its body is overcome by shakes, shudders, tremors. The child is invaded by an excess that cannot be controlled. There are no words that can possibly define what is happening. Language cannot tame this dark sensation of danger that invades the child's body, as happens in certain films (just think of the *Alien* series) when the human body is invaded by a monstrous being that grows inside it like a parasite that grows in the body as it devours it.

The feverish child abandoned in the dark night has nothing but its *scream*. It is through this scream that life turns to the Other in search of support, without which it would be lost. The child is still not able to speak, to explain itself, to ask for help. It cannot see, cannot talk, cannot explain; it has only a confused perception of the body. The child does not know where it is. It is no longer protected by the warmth of the placenta, by the warmth of life in the womb or by the maternal embrace.

It finds itself thrown out, exposed to life, and all of this chaos takes the expressive form of the scream. We are born through a scream as the manifestation of the absolute abandonment into which our lives are thrown. And it is only the response of the Other that makes the signifying translation of the answered scream possible. This is the Other's first task: to translate that scream into a demand for love. The Bible captures this position well in Abraham's response to his Lord: 'Here I am!'[6] We are at the very root of the experience of recognition. Life is not simply a headless drive, a 'will to live' – as Schopenhauer would say – but also, and from the outset, from the moment in which it comes into being, an appeal, an invocation, a prayer to the Other.[7] Life demands the presence of the Other, of the Other as saviour, as Freud had already said, of the neighbour (*Nebenmensch*) who is able to respond to the scream in which life reveals itself, because without the response of the Other life dies, it is dehumanized, it thrashes about in the dark, remaining pure animal life.[8]

Nothing demonstrates the extent to which human life does not consist only of itself but is integrally suspended to the response of the Other like the experience of abandonment. The Christian experience of the crucifix is one of the strongest, most moving expressions of this truth. The dying son calls to his father in heaven without receiving an immediate response: 'My God, My God, why have you forsaken me?' (Mark 15:34, Matthew 27:46).[9] Jesus on the cross is a pure scream, a shout, an appeal to the Other. And, as such, he lives the traumatic experience of receiving no response from the Other. On that cross he experiences the absolute abandonment that he had already faced in his agonizing solitude at Gethsemane.

The Christian experience of the cross reiterates the extent to which the heart of human life lies within the scream, as it is in the scream that life is exposed, a naked life, life without foundations, life exposed to the unlimited contingency of life. And it is only the response of the Other that can translate that scream into a demand for love and humanize life by saving it from the pitch-black night. When, however, this response is lacking, when the Other does not respond, when the scream remains unheard, left to echo in the silence of the night, the process of humanization of life stops, and life emerges as life deprived of meaning, life thrown away, life lost.[10]

Lacan strongly insisted on the decisive nature of the Other's response as the thing that attributes a retroactive meaning to existence, offering it a symbolic citizenship. This is the first form that human love assumes beyond the Freudian schema of narcissistic infatuation: the active gift of the response, of presence, of listening that transforms the scream into word. By responding to the subject's appeal, the Other does not limit itself to dealing with the satisfaction of its basic needs – eating, drinking, being kept warm, clean and cared for – but takes on the subject's desire to feel recognized by the Other as human life, like a word that can only find its meaning when it is heard by the Other. This means that the Other-saviour is not only the Other that looks after the body – the Other of care – but also the Other who responds with its own desire to the desire to be desired by the Other. There is a basic difference between the demand for love and the demand for care. In this sense, Lacan can maintain that love is giving the Other that which one does not have.[11] Limiting oneself to giving what one has would mean responding solely on the level of having, and not that of being. Giving what one does not have means giving the Other the lack that life opens up within us. It means recognizing the unique, unrepeatable, irreplaceable position the Other's life occupies within our own. It means giving the Other not what we have, but giving the lack that their particular life has opened up in us. This is the symbolic power contained in the response to the scream. Where there is a response, exposure to the responsibility for the word, life is no longer in a state of absolute abandonment; it is no longer a coincidence but is wanted, desired, expected. This is why psychoanalysis insists on reiterating how parenthood is always adoptive. It is never natural. It is not a biological given, but requires a symbolic gesture, an act of adoption, the recognition of life through the word: 'Yes! You are my daughter, my son!' Neither the sperm nor the egg, nor the continuation of the blood line, is able to constitute this 'Yes!' The only possible foundation for this 'Yes!' lies in the absolute gesture of responsibility that is, above all, an act of recognition: 'Yes! You are my son, my daughter!' It is this act that humanizes life, allowing it to be associated with meaning.[12]

The Discussion about Barolo

Lacan's second step beyond Freud revolves around the idea that man and woman are two unknown universes that speak two different languages. There is no complementarity, no unity, no harmony: One wants to enjoy the body, the Other wants to enjoy the words. One wants the fetishistic detail, the Other the love letter. One would want all women, the Other would want to be the only one. There can be no possible agreement between these two parallel universes. They appear to Lacan like Achilles and the tortoise in Zeno's famous paradox. The slowest animal and the fastest man on the earth are destined to never reach one another. To make yourself be loved as the only one, and desiring the erotic detail of the body that causes desire, are the feminine and masculine way of entering an amorous discourse and failing at the sexual relationship. No matter how they try, the Two will never be One. The risk is rather that of reciprocal mutilation: the woman can be overcome by the idiocy of her demand for love, which is infinitely repeated because no response will ever satisfy her ('Do you love me?', 'Do you love me?'), whilst the man can be sucked in by the equally rigid idiocy of his fetishistic fantasy and remain enslaved by pieces of the Other's body ('Let's fuck!', 'Let's fuck!').

During a brief holiday in the Langhe a few years ago, upon leaving one of the many wine-tasting courses my wife and I had attended there, I overheard a conversation between a number of women who, like me, had just participated in an interesting lesson on Barolo. One of these confided a fantasy of hers to the others: 'Just think, wouldn't it be great if there were a wine course that limited itself to discussing the perfumes and qualities of the wine without us having to actually taste them?' I could not resist intervening and, addressing them in an amused tone,

I said that only a woman could imagine something like that: tasting words about wine as opposed to tasting the wine itself.

We can freeze-frame two diametrically opposed examples of sexuation in this exchange on the tasting: words of love in place of making love, the sign of the lack in place of the sexual consumption of the body. It was my last comment that amused the small group of women to whom I was talking: 'a man would probably dream of being able to go straight to the wine tasting without the hindrance of words: going straight to the substance, to the sexual body, without passing through the superfluous'.

The Sexual Relationship Does Not Exist

Faced with the abyss that separates the parallel universes of man and woman, love can be *the only* substitute capable of bringing One into a relationship with Another, or rather, of placing each of the Two in a relationship with that which it is impossible to have a relationship with. In this sense, love is not in any way an escape from sexuality but a way of entering into an erotic relationship with the Other without expecting to appropriate their otherness. The most surprising thing about love is, in fact, that it makes the relationship between Two possible, starting precisely with the objection to the notion that the enjoyment of the One is the same as the enjoyment of the Other. This objection consists of the fact that in the sexual encounter it is one's own fantasy that one enjoys the most. The enjoyment of the One always finds itself between the Two, hindering their relationship. In any case, love, instead of dying, finds life in this obstacle. It does not aim for the sexual relationship to exist as an idea of fusion and permeation of One into the Other, but it makes the Two possible, the absolute exposure of each one to the desire and the body of the Other. In other words, the possibility of love is given by the impossibility for each of the Two to overcome their own solitude (which is also the solitude of the other that causes the desire). However, it is precisely this solitude that animates the possibility of establishing not *the* relationship but *a* relationship between the One and the Other. In this sense, love is not an exorcism of the thorny real of sexuality. If this were the correct interpretation of Lacan's line that '*love is a substitute for the non-existence of the sexual relationship*', we could deduce that love is nothing more than a neurotic way of defending oneself from the sexual relationship, and not its most powerful expression.[13] Conversely, love as a substitute for the non-existence of the sexual relationship signifies the possibility of entering into a relationship with that which remains entirely Other, with what exceeds the enjoyment of the One and the narcissistic image of our I. This means that if Achilles will never be able to reach the tortoise, if between man and woman there is no possibility of writing the stable and secure formula of their relationship, if this relationship is exposed to an absolute contingency, the loving bond between the One and the Other must be reinvented each time, constructed and experienced against a background of the impossibility of making and being One with the Other. This is the profound truth of love. It replaces the non-existence of the sexual relationship not because it reconnects lovers, but because it allows them to have a new experience of the world, to experience the suspension of time within time, the eternal in the future, the world in the renewed and unique vision of the Two. Though it may be true that Two never make One, this never making One is the greatest beauty of love: to be in a relationship with what escapes every relationship, being in the Two that eludes the One.[14]

We Are Loved Not Because of Something, But 'Because of Everything'

Let's ask ourselves: what is it we love in the Other? In analysis, when a patient attempts to describe the reasons for their amorous choices, the characteristics they attribute to their beloved always seem inadequate for explaining the reason for their love. No characteristic will ever be capable of summing up what we truly love in the Other because what we love cannot be reduced to a circumscribed aspect of their being. This is the truth with love. We love the Other not because of something they possess, but for their whole being, for their most particular detail, for their own name, as Lacan would say.[15] In short, we love the Other for what escapes us, what we cannot appropriate. We love the Other in their absolute difference, not because of something, but 'because of everything'. 'Because of everything' means because of their fingers, their lips, their smell, their quirks, the colour of their hair, their style, their voice, their attitudes and so on. We do not love the ideal image of our I, but that which constitutes the most particular detail of the Other, that which renders them irreplaceable, 'priceless, 'invaluable', as Jean-Luc Nancy would say,[16] so never because of something but 'because of everything'.[17] Knowing 'everything' about the life of the Other is not simply the desire to see our love reciprocated, but the urge to enter the Other's world, to break the narcissistic screen: to love is not simply to let oneself be loved, but to love, to admire, to look at the world of the Other, to learn that Another world exists, to learn the power of the Two beyond the One.

The Loving Encounter is the Birth of a World

The love of the promise does not fall from heaven. It is not written in the stars nor is it destiny. It will only be able to fall from heaven, be written in the stars or be a destiny retroactively, only in the future perfect tense, *if it will have been, if it will have been revealed* as the love of promise. In this sense, love, even the most absolute, is always exposed to the equally absolute contingency of the encounter. We are well aware of this. No natural necessity determines the loving encounter. Before the loving encounter, love does not exist. It is only the encounter that brings the beloved and the lover into existence as if they had a second life, or another life, which was everything that preceded the event of the encounter. For this reason, Lacan, unlike Freud who thought that everything was already written in the unconscious, invited us to think of the unconscious in the future tense, as that which has not yet been realized, has not yet happened. Not only as a programme that has already been written and demands repetition, but as an opening, a jump forward towards that which has not yet happened.

The loving encounter coincides with the birth of a world, because it constitutes a relationship that makes the world exist in a new way, or as Badiou would say, 'love is always the possibility of being present at the birth of the world', no longer under the sign of the One, but that of the Two.[18] If the event of love is the event of a contingent encounter that no knowledge can foretell, not even that held by the unconscious, once it has happened the lovers tend to make it exist 'forever', to translate its contingency into necessity. This is why astrologers are frequently consulted in these matters. Lovers want to know whether or not the stars really can confirm their hopes that this love *will be forever*. In every love, therefore, we have a fundamental transformation in which the contingency of the event of the encounter becomes a necessary destiny. This is what Sartre believed to be the true joy of love.[19] It consists of the fact that through the Other's love I am saved from my facticity (*facticité*), which, in other terms, means that I no longer exist by coincidence, deprived of meaning. I am no longer 'too much' in the world. My existence is not here for no reason, but has become the 'meaning' of the Other's life, that which gives meaning to that life and which from that life reciprocally draws its own significance. This is the joy of love when it exists. Once it is loved, my existence, which is never founded by itself, finds that it exists because it is wanted by the Other in its most minute details, because of 'everything'. It is 'called', it is 'expected'. The demand for love is qualified, therefore, as a *demand for meaning*: I want to be saved by the unbearable weight of my facticity, from the non-sense that accompanies my coming into the world. The Other who loves me removes me from a state of absolute abandonment, giving me new meaning and, in doing so, also attributes a new meaning to the world. The closed world of the One opens up to the new world of the Two. While the beginning of life was dominated by the shapeless chaos of the scream, the absence of meaning, and the pure facticity of existence, now my life is given meaning, feels wanted, desired, justified in its existence. Sartre described it best:

> Where, before we were loved, we were troubled by this unjustified and unjustifiable protuberance that was our existence, where we felt ourselves '*de trop*', now we feel that this existence has been reclaimed and willed, right down to the last detail, by an absolute freedom that is conditioned by it at the same time – and that, along with our own freedom, we are willing ourselves. That is the basis of love's joy, when it exists: to feel ourselves justified in existing.[20]

Loving desire makes an effort to remove human life from its absolute abandonment. It is the attempt, through the Other, to legitimize my very existence, making a second birth possible, allowing the beloved and the world to be born together again, once more, by making the beloved feel 'expected', 'chosen', 'called upon', 'irreplaceable' – signifying their existence from the starting point of an absolute mandate. It is love that, in other words, redeems the brutal and absurd nature of being in the world, retroactively conferring human meaning upon this event. The original futility of existence thus seems to find a necessary foundation through the Other. This is love's most profound joy. It is what Lacan, in the final part of his *Seminar XX*, theorizes as its most proper possibility: *transforming the contingency of the encounter into a need, coincidence into destiny.*[21] My life has been redeemed, its existence is justified, it is wanted in its tiniest details for everything that is. It is still wanted, again, once more.

Disappointed Love

The loving encounter is not an illusion. Rather, it is what causes the illusion of being enough for ourselves, the narcissism of the I and its dream of independence to evaporate. Rather than reinforcing the narcissistic image of the I, it upends it, messes it up, resets it, forcing it to encounter its own limit. The loving encounter does not confirm our identity, but disturbs it, forcing it to be contaminated, to give itself up. It implies a weakening of the I, a loss of control, a loss, the risk of absolute exposure to the unknown of the Other's desire. Whilst in narcissistic illusion the shadow of my fantasy captures me and I am in thrall to it, in the loving encounter I crash into the invisible but absolutely real otherness of the Other. The encounter is, in fact, only an encounter with the *heteros* of the Other, with the most real real of the Other, with that aspect of the Other which escapes every narcissistic specularity, every sentimental symmetry.

When, instead, the illusion acts, it renders the encounter with the Other impossible by projecting onto it the fantasy of our own narcissistic image. In this case, the encounter is not an encounter with the Other because it is made impossible by the unconscious reproduction of the shadow of the Self. Faced with the narcissistic exaltation of the image of the other as an idealized version of that of the I, time acts fatally, causing an erosion (be it slow or sudden) that causes disappointment. Analysis teaches us in the most ruthless way that *the love that is disappointed is often the one that is most idealized.* Freud highlighted how the illusory dimension of falling in love is consumed when faced with the tricks of the mirror.[22] We have already seen this: the I loves and searches for the Other only in its own idealized image. For this reason, upon discovering even the smallest flaw in this image, the loving emphasis can easily evaporate, leaving way for bitter hatred. It does not take much for this to happen: an unexpected cough, the wrong coloured sock, the discovery of particularly large feet, a lack of oral hygiene, an overly protruding nose or one that is too small. It takes very little, very little indeed, for the other to fall from their position as the Ideal and reveal themselves to be naked in their real. In these cases, there is no encounter with the Other, only with the imperfection of our own image, which the Other should have reflected back to us in its most complete way and which instead was reflected back as chipped, inadequate and defective, thus disappointing us.

The Eros of the Encounter

But is there anything that can distinguish the loving encounter from a repetition of that same delusion? Is it possible not to be dazzled by the narcissistic Ideal projected by the Other onto the private screen of our fantasy? Does this misunderstanding not always occur? Do we not perhaps encounter the Other through the deforming and disoriented lens of our unconscious fantasy? How can we distinguish between the otherness of the Other and the shadow of our maternal or paternal fantasy? How can an encounter interrupt rather than encourage its repetition?

The loving encounter is never idyllic. It does not extinguish the fetishism that guides the male fantasy, or the erotomania that guides the female fantasy. In this sense, every love experiences the partiality of the object. And yet, it also knows how to exceed both the fetishism of the body and the erotomania of the demand for love. In the loving encounter, the object is no longer just any object, it is no longer the means for the drive to be satisfied, nor is it any longer just a partial object – *object small a* in Lacan's algebra, the object that causes sexual desire.[23] At the forefront, there is now the actual name of the subject, their particular being. And love aims at this, it aims at loving 'everything' of the Other, loving their very being and making loving desire converge with their own body's drive to enjoy. This convergence means that the metonymical course of desire from one object to another can finally stop. This is why, according to Lacan, '*encore*', as we have already seen, is the best word with which to say love. It means that the encounter requires repetition, it needs to happen again, once more, again, *encore* 'forever'. *The object is not replaced with another object, but appears as irreplaceable.* The *encore* of the demand for love mysteriously insists on the same object, it does not move from there, it wants its infinite repetition. It is '*encore*' not in the sense of the New, as the libertine ideology of our time would have it, but in the sense of the Same that becomes New. It is not a demand for another Thing, but always for the same thing as it is Other. This is the 'infinite in action' of which love consists.[24] The sexual enjoyment of the body is married to the desire of the Other or, to be more precise, the impersonality of the object *a* that attracts me – the breasts, the legs, the gaze, the lips, the hands, etc. – merges with the irreplaceability, the absolute untranslatable nature, the not-me of the beloved.[25] It is what happens in every love: the very name of the beloved takes on the density and the substance of a body, it is eroticized, becoming a carnal signifier and, at the same time, the body takes on the same symbolic value of the name, appearing at times unique, untranslatable, irreplaceable, different from all others, incomparable.[26]

This is why the loving encounter is, before all else, an encounter between bodies, but not without the Other. The body is not simply fragmented in a fetishistic manner, but wanted because of what it expresses about the Other's being. It is interesting to note how the word 'again' in French – *encore* – sounds rather like '*un corps*', a body. Without the eroticism of bodies, love would risk being reduced to a mere defence against sexual desire, a spiritualist idealism. Yet without the abandonment of the Other, the unreserved absolute exposure to the Other, without the gift of oneself, the yielding of one's own I, without the love for the Other's being, it would risk deteriorating into an Eros blinded by the purely fetishistic power of the object.

Strictly speaking, there is no encounter without it being an erotic encounter or, put differently, the encounter of love is always erotic,[27] and this erotic dimension surpasses the neurotic opposition between sexual desire and the offering of oneself to the Other, as it does not detach but causes love to converge through the particularity of the Other's being with the sexual enjoyment of its body. This is not an illusion. This love exists and increases over time. It is the encounter that broadens life, it satisfies the body, eroticizes the world, renders desire non-hysterical. It is an encounter that opens at once the drives of orifices and worlds.

Fidelity

The loving encounter is not content with happening just once, but wants to repeat. It wants to return, it wants to be 'forever', it wants infinite repetition, or rather the infinite in the act of repetition. In this sense, love becomes word, a pact, a promise, faith. It wants to transform the contingency of the encounter into a necessity. By doing so, it reveals its proximity to the infinite. What has happened between us cannot end, it cannot exhaust itself here but demands to return once more; it insists that it be again, once more, *encore* forever. It is fidelity that introduces a fragment of eternity into the passing of time, transforming coincidence into destiny. For this reason and this reason only, not for any moralistic ones, fidelity is an essential attitude in love. Remaining the Same, still wanting the Same to find the Other, the New in that Same, not to lose oneself in the aleatory capture of the New as opposed to the Same.[28] However, if fidelity to the loving Other fed the cult of sacrifice, if it imposed itself as a must-be, if it served to forestall the ever-possible encounter with an Other, if it fed the mortification of life, it would not be fidelity but a masochistic relinquishing of desire. It would be nothing more than the sad expression of the senseless tyranny of the Super-Ego, a neurotic subjugation determined by the need to avoid and demonize desire. We would be faced with fidelity as a symptom and not a choice. This kind of degradation of fidelity is regularly the subject of psychoanalytic treatment. I remember once, at the beginning of my analytic training, listening to a debate by analysts on this very subject: can analysis help to liberate the subject from the burden of fidelity or to make fidelity possible? It was evident that there was no unequivocal answer to that question. Fidelity is such only if it is an event of freedom, if it is a choice of desire. If, instead, it becomes a straitjacket, it does not support the subject's desire, only its super-egoic punishment.

Being faithful to the encounter means still wanting it. Not removing oneself from the absolute risk that it brings. One of my patients, who could not decide between his wife and his lover, carried on his unconscious the indelible wound of a mother who, without a word of warning, abandoned their home when he was still a child. How was it possible to have faith in the Other if the Other betrays, if their presence cannot be trusted? In this case, infidelity became for him, paradoxically, a phobic protection against his anxiety of being abandoned by those he truly loved. Having more than one single woman protected him from the risk of the repetition of loss, but also hindered his access to an absolute exposure to love.

Fidelity as renunciation misunderstands the meaning of the Law because it experiences the Law as a burden to which it must submit rather than as a support for desire. Conversely, fidelity founded on the pact of the word and the promise experiences the Law as a liberation of desire. It wants this Other about whom I love everything, the entirety of whose real I welcome, this living Other who is irreducible to any ideal, to stay with me forever. This fidelity refuses self-sacrifice. It is not the concealment of my urge to cheat, it is not the manifestation of a repressive mortification of life, but it involves the exposure to love as an act in which I play my entire life. No emergency back-ups. This is what my patient cannot give up. He keeps himself perennially divided between his wife and his lover to avoid the repetition of the trauma of abandonment and to ward off his own phallic insufficiency.

The Face and the Eternal

The 'forever' love that tends towards an absolute exposure to the desire of the Other highlights the irreplaceable nature of the particular existence of the beloved. This exposure does not simply define the relationship between a couple. For example, in the traumatized and Godless world of *The Road* by Cormac McCarthy it also runs through the relationship between father and son. The love that binds them does not only resist the triumph of evil, but it gives them back a sense of their own existence in the world. Love is never just a private relationship between the Two because it implies an openness to a new world. Rather, it is the very face of a child – in this case, of the son – that makes the possibility of God exist, that renders the very meaning of the world possible once more. In theological terms we should say (at the risk of committing blasphemy?) that it is the face of the creature that allows for the foundation of the possibility of the Creator. Isn't it in this way that we meet the faces of the ones we love? Is this not how they are presented to us – in time and in history – as a fragment of eternity that suspends time despite being in time? It is a fact, and a psychological experiment that we can easily conduct on ourselves: we never get tired of looking at the face of the person we love. Love that does not remain narcissistically hypnotized by the image turns towards the being, towards that finite and real existence of the Other. For this reason it is tied to the unique detail of that face, that body, that name. As a principle of exteriority and alterity, as Levinas would say, the face is truly transfigured into an absolute and time is suspended. 'I would like this to be forever' is the absolute promise of the lover, their glorious strength that requires no compensation.[29]

The face of the loved one is the Same but always New. Ulysses refuses the gift of immortality offered to him by the nymph in order to see the beloved faces of Telemachus and Penelope. In *The Road* it is the child's face, the face of the son that saves the possibility of God the Creator. The face of my child or of the one I love that I see every morning and at the end of each night, that I see again, day after day, *encore*, is that not perhaps the only face of the eternal that I am allowed to contemplate in this world? The vertical relationship between the Creator and the created seems to be inverted here. Is this not another great (Christian?) love lesson that wants to be absolute, that does not retreat when faced with the absolute character of their exposure to the Other? While Augustine maintained that the principal form of sin consisted in loving the Creator's creations more intensely than the Creator himself, today, in this time of the pure absence of the Law, of the death of God, of the evaporation of the father, in this time of the 'night of the Proci', in this time that is witnessing God's retreat from the world, today when the proposition of a hierarchical, vertical representation of God would have no meaning whatsoever, now that we are forced to rethink the father from the ground up, should we not also reconsider the relationship between the Creator and the created?[30] Should we not perhaps make love for the created the condition for the possibility of once more attributing meaning to the world? Is love not perhaps that which absolutely saves the created in their boundless freedom?

We never get tired of seeing the face of our loved one, we would want to see it forever, over and over again, because in the finite nature of that face the infinite in its entirety is expressed. It is the limit of every human love: how can an infinite love exist if our life is finite? I have always asked myself, thinking of the Christian mystery of resurrection, why I would want to preserve my existence if I would no longer be able to see the face of the person I have loved on this earth. As if the created had the same absolute value for me as the Creator. Love only tends towards the absolute by virtue of the created. Is this not the central significance of the Christian God's making himself human, of his incarnation, of the face of Jesus – followed by, or rather, simultaneously with, that of the neighbour – as the only possibility of encountering the face of the Father?

3

Trauma and Abandonment

A Captive Freedom?

Every lover carries within them a plan to hold their beloved captive. But this plan is different from those that aim for a simple possessive suppression of freedom. When there is love, one does not love the beloved as a prisoner, but because of the strength and freedom that their image and presence provoke in us. That which we truly love of the Other is always their independence, their otherness, their being *heteros*. In this sense, the beloved's freedom seems to know no master. And yet the lover, despite all of their love for the freedom of the one they love, would also like to be its custodian, the only holder of that freedom. There is nothing scandalous about this: loving desire is transfixed by this internal ambiguity that Sartre pinpointed as the most profound paradox of love. There is an urge to possess the beloved object and this urge belongs to love, but the lover would not simply like to possess something of the Other, but their very *freedom*. It is at this point that the paradox opens: how is it possible to possess the Other as an absolute freedom that is, at the same time, captive? How is it possible for a captive freedom to exist?

The lover would want the beloved's absolute freedom to be not an effect of imprisonment, but the result of a free choice that would know how to constantly renew that promise. The dream of every love is held within this paradoxical desire: to possess the Other, but only if they are free. But how can one possess the Other without ending their freedom? How can something like a 'captive freedom' exist?

It is precisely because nothing akin to a captive freedom can exist that each love is exposed to the risk of the end. And the love that does not use the narcissistic cement that would want to unite the One with the Other is exposed to an even greater risk. Non-narcissistic love is not founded on the confusion between the One and the Other, but on the reciprocal solitude of the Two. This is why the Two are always called upon to decide whether or not to renew their promise. They are, in other words, always free to leave one another.

The lover does not simply demand the sexual body of the beloved. Love cannot be reduced to the fetishistic desire of the 'piece' of the Other's body. The eroticism of love runs through the body but is never fully consumed by it. Rather, it floods the world. Love always opens up a new world and this opening, of which the truth of love consists, provides new foundations for its existence, causing it to be born, as it were, once more. In this sense, the demand for love always implies, and always transcends, the enjoyment of the body. It demands the sign of the *Other's desire*. The lover does not desire 'something' of the Other – it does not limit itself to demand the presence of the phallus, or of the object *a* according to Lacan's theory – but desires to be *desired* by the Other. It desires to be the desire that is desired by the Other. It desires the sign that it is the cause of the Other's lack.[1] For this reason, the lover is never focusing solely on the Other-object, the body of the Other, but the object contained within the body of the Other in itself already acts as an index of the Other as a subject, an expression of its most personal freedom, of its most particular being. In other words, returning to the paradox illustrated by Sartre, it is the freedom of the beloved that the lover wishes to appropriate. They do not simply desire to possess the beloved as they possess any old thing, but they intend to exercise 'a special type of appropriation'. Hence, they want 'to possess a freedom as freedom'.[2] They want the beloved to be *freely theirs*. They do not want the beloved to be their prisoner – love is not an effect of constriction – and they cannot bear reducing the loved subject to a tool of their own enjoyment. The lover's design is more intricate and, as we have seen, paradoxical: they want to reach the heart of the Other, their freedom, they want this freedom – the beloved's freedom – to be entirely theirs. They want the beloved to be *free and captive* at the same time.

Albertine

In Proust's novel *In Search of Lost Time* we find a compelling description of the paradox that runs through the urge to appropriate, which inhabits loving desire. The plan adopted by the novel's protagonist in order to exercise absolute possession of his loved one, Albertine, has the opposite effect to the one he had in mind. He realizes that the isolation of his beloved will never be fully achieved given that the Other is, as such, irreducible to any plan of assimilation, for they evade any plan to appropriate. Albertine is the pure image of the Other's transcendence. 'Even when you hold them in your hands', Proust writes of Albertine,

> such persons are fugitives. To understand the emotions which they arouse, and which others, even better looking, do not, we must recognise that they are not immobile, but in motion, and add to their person a sign which corresponds to that which in physics denotes speed.[3]

The most paradoxical point is that this irreducibility emerges precisely when his efforts to isolate her succeed. If, in fact, the lover loses that feature of freedom, it causes the passion of loving desire to fail. Once Albertine has been taken prisoner, her lover's desire experiences a sudden decline, it fails, collapses. For him, Albertine is no longer the incarnation of a transcendence, but becomes just another object, losing any agalmatic value as something to be worshipped or exalted. The distance that institutes difference, *heteros*, that feeds the urge of desire, fails. Marcel is thus forced to discover that if he demands his beloved is his and, at the same time, continues to exist as a freedom, as the incarnation of a transcendence, then he is asking the impossible. Though his aim was to possess Albertine's freedom, isolating her, making her a prisoner, he actually finds himself faced with nothing more than a lifeless body, an inert, dead object. He realizes that he cannot make the possessed body of the Other adhere to his most intimate freedom without any deviation. A metamorphosis has rendered his beloved unrecognizable. The prisoner is no longer the Other-subject that Marcel wanted to possess, but an Other-object which no longer holds any interest for him:

> It was no longer the same Albertine, because she was not, as at Balbec, incessantly in flight upon her bicycle, impossible to find owing to the number of little watering-places where she would go to spend the night with friends and where moreover her lies made it more difficult to lay hands upon her; because, shut up in my house, docile and alone, she was no longer what at Balbec, even when I had succeeded in finding her, she used to be on the beach, that fugitive, cautious, deceitful creature, whose presence was expanded by the thought of all those assignations which she was skilled in concealing, which made one love her because they made one suffer, [. . .] because the sea breeze no longer puffed out her skirts; because, above all, I had clipped her wings, and she had ceased to be a winged Victory, and had become a burdensome slave of whom I would have liked to rid myself.[4]

Imprisoning his beloved no longer allows him to possess her freedom as such. Rather, it reveals Albertine to be a worthless slave, because love needs the Other to be free. Marcel's disappointment, like that of all lovers who imprison their own loves in forced bonds out of jealousy, is similar to that of the child who takes apart an alarm clock in order to find time, but actually finds nothing but cogs and gears.[5] It is as if beneath the skin, at the heart of the Other's body, of their having been imprisoned, hidden away, there remained a presence that was still latent, irreducible, always *heteros*, and impossible to grasp. It is a presence that is maintained in a kind of oblivion surpassing the confines of the body from the inside. It does not allow itself to be touched, it cannot be captured, it maintains a position of maximum transcendence despite being there, entirely mixed in with and entirely immanent in the body of the Other.

> We imagine that it [love] has as its object a being that can be laid down in front of us, enclosed within a body. Alas, it is the extension of that being to all the points in space and time that it has occupied and that it will occupy. [. . .] But we cannot touch all those points.[6]

We would all like to love a captive freedom: I don't want you to be mine because I hold you in a prison, I don't want you to be mine because when I leave the house I lock you inside. I want you to be mine because you freely desire it, because you are free to want to be so, and as such to decide to only be mine, dedicated exclusively to me. Every lover would like the Other to be able to renew their absolute fidelity whilst being absolutely free.

Is the Promise of Love Always False?

Nothing ensures that promises of love are kept, nothing guarantees the absolute truth of love. The loving encounter occurs in the purest contingency. It is always within the order of the unexpected, the unforeseen, surprise. And yet, this event demands faithful repetition; it wants to continue to exist in time, it wants to be forever but nothing can guarantee that it will last. This is another paradox that envelops lovers. The truth of their love that they feel to be entirely evident, resistant to both time and history, in reality has no protection. It is, as Lacan would say, without an Other of the Other that might be able to justify it.[7] No symbolic pact – not even that of marriage – can protect them from its aleatory nature. This is another way of saying that every loving bond occurs against a backdrop of the non-existence of the sexual relationship. Nothing, no Other, no God can guarantee that it will be 'forever'. In this sense, the absolute exposure to love is always an absolute risk.

So, are the promises made by lovers always false? Are they a trap? Are they ways to ward off the random nature of human bonds? Does their vow carry with it, as Jacques Derrida would seem to have believed, the inevitable nature of the liar?[8] How is it possible to suspend time, to say first what we will do or what we will be, without excluding the possibility of change? How is it possible, they say, to stake a claim on the future? Is every promise that wants to be forever not necessarily false, destined to be betrayed? Is every marriage – founded on the symbolic pact of the word – not a purely Christian folly?[9]

The experience of great love demonstrates how the promise can bind lovers in time and beyond time. It is the obstinacy of desire that wants the Same to be New each time. It is the '*encore*' of the demand for love, its infinite at work. The word that declares the promise – 'it will be forever' – certainly has no guarantee other than the truth for which it manages to vouch. The foundation of the promise can only be in the unfounded foundation of one's own word given to the Other. No God, no Other can sustain the truth of this word. No one can guarantee how long the love will last. And yet, we are well aware that the word always transforms the person who welcomes it. 'You are my wife!', as Lacan deftly demonstrated, is a statement that touches my being, transforming it completely, making me 'husband', binding me to a symbolic pact that transcends me, modifying the very structure of my existence.[10]

'It's Not Like It Used To Be'

As such, even great loves, the love of one's life, can end. Usually the crisis in a relationship begins with the communication by one of the Two, or the recognition by both, that 'it's not like it used to be', that something has been corroded by time, that a deterioration of desire has taken place. Our time, the time of the libertine cult of the New, wants to make this situation an iron-clad law that allows no exceptions. One begins a relationship already convinced that, sooner or later, they are going to witness its death throes. Love ends due to a depletion of its forward momentum, or because of the appearance of another object, or a combination of both. It is quite something to note how it is increasingly rare for someone who experiences a significant emotional separation to interrupt the loss of the object with a pause of solitude, rather than rushing to replace them with a new object. This is also an effect of the manic rhythm that rules both our collective lives and those that are intimately emotional. But what happens when the love of our lives is overwhelmed by loss and separation? That very love that had the power to suspend time, to repeat itself over again, again like today, the Same again? What happens when the phrase 'it's not like it used to be' is said by the person who, up until that moment, was the presence who gave meaning to our own presence in the world? What happens when this communication does not signal simply the failure of the narcissistic splendour of the image, but shakes our entire world, making it teeter and leaving us feeling lost, abandoned, plunged once more into the darkness of the night?

What Is a Trauma?

The trauma of abandonment, as psychoanalytic practice demonstrates, rekindles the oldest, primary traumas, taking the subject back to those wounds from long ago. The trauma does not only invade the body but, most significantly, psychological life. It is an event that causes the walls of our identity to break down and that destroys the certainty on which our life is built. In the case of the sexual abuse that upends the life of a twelve-year-old girl, for example, the trauma does not lie solely in having been brutally made the object of the Other's enjoyment, but consists above all in the encounter with an unexpected transfiguration of the face of the Other. The relative who has abused her was someone she knew well, a friendly figure, an Other whom the girl innocently trusted. In the trauma of abuse, this figure suddenly changes, revealing themselves to be a bad Other who wants to enjoy the subject. We see the same condition in the protagonist in the Greek film by Alexandros Avranas, *Miss Violence* (2013), a family's youngest sister who is initiated into prostitution by her incestuous father-grandfather in whom, up until that point, the child had placed all of her trust. Her most profound drama is not that of falling into the hands of a stranger who rapes her, but of having been placed in those hands by the very person whom she trusted most, who had been entrusted with protecting her life. In this case, the trauma of abuse is not only the predatory violence that tortures a girl's body, but it is most significantly the trauma of the collapse of trust in the Other. The family bond as a place that safeguards life is turned upside down, becoming something that threatens her, brutally defiling her. The certainty of the family as a protected place, a root, a signifier of belonging, makes way for an unknown face that reveals itself to be monstrous. The symbolic certainty on which life is sustained is shaken to its very foundations by the emergence of a real without a name. In this sense, the trauma is not just and not so much a trauma of the body, but a trauma of life that loses faith in the Other as the place of its foundation. Even in the case of my young patient, the encounter with the 'monster' takes place in the family where, for the culture in which she was raised, 'everything is sacred'. It is not only the abused body that is afflicted by a serious eating disorder, but the subject's entire bond with the world is damaged. The certainty that had pushed her to trust her family up to that point has been smashed to pieces. With the significant addition that the girl's admission of the abuse to which she had been subjected provokes no outrage in her mother, who instead advises her abused daughter to undertake a sort of *omertà*-like silence to protect the conformist order of family relations. For this child it will never be like it used to be. Not only her body, but most of all her relationship with the Other is upended, because the mother's word, rather than sustaining her own, orders her silence, forcing her into the position of the passive object in the hands of the Other.

We find the same structure of trauma in another clinical case. In this case, the subject is the victim of a terrorist attack. Having been raised in a very Catholic family that has always striven to see all those around them as worthy of love and respect, he finds himself in the midst of a bloodbath caused by an exploding bomb. The tranquillity of the exclusive resort in which he was staying was interrupted by the deafening sound caused by the explosion and the 'beastly' screaming of the people who had been hit. This ferocious and unforeseeable event not only breaks the rhythm of a calm holiday abroad, but splinters his faith in his neighbours, the faith in the Other that the group culture to which he belonged had placed at the very heart of his experience in the world. A new and terrifying face of the Other appears through the smoke and corpses produced by the bomb. This is what constitutes the heart of the trauma: an event that punctures the established order of the world insofar as it causes the cornerstone constituted by certainty and faith in the Other to falter.[11]

In Giulia's case it was jealousy that made her life impossible. All of her loving relationships were marked by the same difficulty in trusting the Other who, exasperated, would eventually leave her. Jealousy had accompanied her throughout her life like a shadow, but where had it come from? As a young girl the person she had always thought to be her father told her one day that he was not, and that she was the result of a relationship her mother had had with another man, who had abandoned her straight after her birth. Her sensation was that every time she entrusted herself to someone she risked not only losing the object of her love but also herself, with no possibility of finding herself again. The fixed time of the trauma incessantly repeated the scene of the original untrustworthy nature of the paternal Other.

The First Blow

In Jean Améry's testimony about the torture inflicted upon him by the Nazis, the acute moment of the trauma, its emergence, does not so much lie in the violence suffered by his body, but in that first slap, that first hit, that first blow. Why? Because it is this blow that rips through the Other's veil, revealing their traumatic alteration. With this first blow, that which Améry already knew – the inhumane nature of the Nazis – became a reality, inscribed without any mediation on his living flesh. The trauma occurs with that first blow because it is the first blow that dismantles the image of the Other as trustworthy, a saviour. Of course, in a sense, it was already entirely evident: falling into the hands of the Nazis never meant falling into the hands of a trustworthy Other. But there was the singular shock of that first blow that retroactively illuminated the entire scene as a terrifying disappearance of the subject, his reduction to a defenceless object in the hands of the Other, his being plunged into the most absolute abandonment. No Other could respond to his cry again:

> The first blow brings home to the prisoner that he is *helpless*, and thus it already contains in the bud everything that is to come. One may have known about torture and death in the cell [. . .] but upon the first blow they are anticipated as real possibilities, yes, as certainties. They are permitted to punch me in the face, the victim feels in numb surprise and concludes in just as numb certainty: they will do with me what they want. Whoever would rush to the prisoner's aid – a wife, a mother, a brother or friend – he won't get this far. [. . .] At the first blow, however, trust in the world breaks down. The other person *opposite* whom I exist physically in the world and *with* whom I can only exist as long as he does not touch my skin surface as border, forces his own corporeality on me with the first blow. He is on me and thereby destroys me. It is like a rape, a sexual act without the consent of one of the two partners.[12]

The abandonment to one's self coincides with the abandonment to the hands of an Other who is no longer the location of the commandment that forbids murder, but an Other who can kill, who does not reassure life but who threatens and humiliates it. There is no help, no mother, no brother, no friend who can respond to the scream of the subject who has fallen into the hands of a mad Other. With that first blow the entire world collapses, because it is no longer sustained by 'trust'.[13] The Other's enjoyment is manifested here in all of its destructive power: it is pure will to subjugate, rape, abuse, to cancel out any right.

Trauma is the Flipside of Repression

Trauma, like great loves, wants to be forever. This is its curse. It is something that can never be forgotten, that insists on repeating itself and wounding the subject. This is why, for Lacan, trauma is the most appropriate name for the real.[14] It tends to always return to the same place, to oppose any activity of symbolization. The real inertia of the traumatic event opposes the metaphorical work of the symbol in the same way the real repetition opposes the symbolic one of repression. The repetition of trauma operates like a return of the event that is impossible to think of, to say, to symbolize. The temporality of the trauma is, more precisely, that of the *impossibility of oblivion*, of the impossibility of separating oneself from the traumatic event. The memory besieges and never leaves the subject. Its lyric and involuntary nature, described in a sublime way in Proust's novel, is overturned: that which we would like to forget assails us, whilst that which we would like to remember escapes us. In this sense, trauma is *the exact flipside of repression*. With repression a part of memory is detached. It is suspended and something (the part that has been removed) separates from consciousness, so that it does not come to the surface in memory but is subject to amnesia, distancing itself from consciousness in order to present itself only in forms that are encoded – metaphorical, symbolic, symptoms and dreams. In trauma, however, the event can no longer be forgotten. It always returns because it has never been able to be deleted, it has never undergone symbolic repression but rather a *split* that confines it to the zone of the unthinkable. Put simply, the traumatized subject cannot separate itself from what it has experienced. For this reason it is not the dream that causes the return of the traumatic event, but insomnia or nightmares as *failures of the dream* due to an excessive presence of the real. The mark of the traumatic event, of the irreversible fall of the Other, grips the subject; it will not let them forget, it refuses repression. Does the problem, then, become one of subjectivizing this *unthinkable* event? How do we go about inhabiting our own subjectivity which has been unforgettably wounded by trauma?

Trauma in Love

In love, trauma usually takes the form of abandonment and betrayal. In these cases, it is again the face of the Other that changes: that face is not like it was before. The figure that was so sweetly familiar to you, that had waited for your life and given it meaning, now traumatically reveals itself to be a stranger. Everything that had previously brought you joy to remember now torments you, without you being able to manage its spectral existence. As a result, insomnia and nightmares punctuate the nights of those traumatized by love. Eyes wide open in the darkness, the nightmare that jolts you awake, the restless tossing and turning in bed all demonstrate the subject's difficulty in forgetting, in accessing sleep as a place of separation from the incandescence of the traumatic event as the location of the symbolic formation of the dream. There is no rest for the one who has been abandoned.[15] Giving in to sleep, with the help of some drug or other, can alleviate the pain caused by the inescapable memory of the wound left by the betrayal and abandonment. But the fact remains that here, at the very forefront, is the experience of anxiety that is for Lacan the experience of the 'lack of the lack', or rather the impossibility of subtracting oneself from the inexorable returns of the traumatic real.[16] The subject cannot forget, because they are unable to accept the realization that it is not like it used to be. The subject is not able to symbolize the loss of the object of their love, of that object that gave meaning to their experience in the world. Careful: it is not only the subject that falls, that gets lost, that can no longer find itself, but the meaning of the world as it was that fails, falls apart. The world stripped of meaning descends into the absolute violence of non-sense. If love has been the way of attributing meaning to our existence, its loss pushes us back into the abyss of non-sense. In the case of betrayal or abandonment in love, this process of falling into non-sense reaches its peak when the object of trauma *coincides* with the loved object. The source of goodness is transfigured into one of wickedness without giving the subject enough time to understand what is happening.

Falling into Non-Sense

The lovers' promise has no foundation other than the pact of the word. No God, no father, no big Other is able to guarantee that this pact will be everlasting. We have seen this already: it is the mystery and the drama of love. This absolute – this suspension of historic time that results in the infinite '*encore*' of the demand of love – can extinguish itself, it can no longer exist, it can know its end. The traumatic experience of abandonment is the experience of this real cataclysm. Time reappears unavoidably in the ashes of that which is no longer how it used to be, breaking the promise of 'forever'. Now the Other is no longer the one who saves us; they no longer have the face of the Other-as-saviour, but of the one who drowns us mercilessly.

In the trauma of abandonment, the one who ensured absolute good becomes the one who inflicts absolute evil. At play here is not only the interruption of the presence of the Other, but also the collapse of their word and, therefore, their promise. If love saves life by associating it with meaning, the loss of love casts it back into the primitive violence of non-sense. If love saves us from absolute abandonment by virtue of the absolute exposure to the Other's desire, its end coincides with the subject's catastrophic return to that absolute abandonment. In this sense, every love that ends opens the deepest wounds in the one who has been left, in the one who has been exposed to the trauma of the end. And the fact that every love is exposed to the risk of the end does not in any way soften the traumatic impact that the end of a love has on the subject who still loves someone who is no longer there. Because with every end, bar a few exceptions, the same thing happens as when a friend or someone close to us dies: one of us Two will go first, because a synchronous exit from the world is not foreseen, one of the Two will have to witness the Other's disappearance into the land of the dead.

The Fall This Side of the Mirror

The experience of betrayal wounds the lover who wants eternity, because it betrays the word. It betrays the promise that announced the existence of a lasting love. It reveals that in every vow there is always, as Derrida would say, the shadow of deceit, the possibility of betrayal that can never be entirely deactivated.[17] Prenuptial agreements that establish the division of assets in the case of separation are increasingly common today, introducing from the very moment of the symbolic declaration of the pact the provision for its end. The risk of love is softened by security measures before it has even had a chance to be tested. And this risk is the risk of the end, the risk of abandonment that no promise is ever able to forestall.

In the trauma of betrayal and abandonment, life is suddenly led back to this side of the mirror. It has become a life stripped bare, without hope of rescue, deprived of the Other, without an image, without hope. This is why a depressive phase unfailingly accompanies the end of a love story. If in the loving encounter contingency demands repetition, if the salvation of love consists in translating contingency, if the lovers' promise wants to transform the case of their encounter into a destiny, in the experience of abandonment, in the traumatic interruption in the presence of the Other, we fall into the purest of contingencies, we sink into the real of bare life without meaning, we regress to this side of the mirror, to the experience of the fragmented body, to the absence of an image, to the senseless vortex of life. Is this not also a possible definition of trauma? Is there not trauma every time we are violently driven back without symbolic mediation into our primary condition of absolute abandonment, of defencelessness, in the absence of presence? Don't we experience trauma each time we go back to experiencing our lives as a scream lost in the night?

A Wound With No Cure

The wound caused by the trauma of betrayal can at times take on the physical form of a perceived amputation. It is a sign of the special regression to the mirror stage – on this side of the image – that the trauma of abandonment causes to resurface. One of my patients who had discovered an unimaginable betrayal by his wife saw himself in a post-traumatic dream in a mirror with a prosthetic arm. He knew that under the prosthesis the amputated arm was no longer there, that he had lost it forever. However, as happens with the phantom limb phenomenon, he could feel the pain of the amputation as if it were happening in precisely that moment. In the mirror, his image appeared normal – the state to which his life with his wife returned after a brief period of turbulence – but he carried on his body the marks of the traumatic event, the resurfacing of the real castration that had struck him. His absent arm still caused him pain, as if the cut were repeating through every moment of his life.

We could ask ourselves, is there a 'phantom limb phenomenon' in the trauma of betrayal? It is certainly the case that those who have been betrayed have a different perception of their bodies, painful, mutilated somehow, of a body that is fragmenting, of falling onto this side of the narcissistic image. The loss of trust in the Other leaves its mark. Can the offence be unforgettable? Can it continue to exist even if it has been overcome through forgiveness? In my patient's dream the amputated limb is no longer there, yet it continues to be painful. Is this perhaps the indelible residue of the trauma – to feel pain each time the thought of the betrayal resurfaces? Nothing can cancel out the trauma of the wound. In fact, its deletion usually responds to the defence mechanisms found in the imaginary split rather than as a result of symbolic introjection. One of my patients, having discovered her beloved husband's infidelity, brought to the sessions a number of dreams whose recurring theme was her wounded body, or rather, her body open like an enormous wound, a wound – as she herself described it – 'with no possible cure'. In her dream, each time she tried to suture the wound that would appear on some part of her body, it would grow, extending itself in an irregular way over the entire surface of her body until it terrifyingly became one with the body itself.

Abandonment

Abandonment is not just the experience of a fall from the world's stage, because the world continues to exist as it did before despite no longer being the same. This is what is experienced by lovers exposed to the trauma of abandonment. Everything is like it was before: the streets, the shop windows, the clothes, the face, the hands, the cinemas, the restaurants, the books, the weather, the mornings, the nights, the light of day, the bus stops, the friends, the shoes, the pictures, the glasses, the cups, the body itself. Everything remains the same, and yet nothing is like it used to be. The presence of the world has been inter-rupted. The inundation of trauma exists, even if it is invisible, and it shakes the entire foundations of the world as we knew it through the eyes of the Two. In abandonment, the world becomes like the wreck of a ship that you had known before in its time of glory. It is a real time of mourning: the world continues to be as it was before but the absence of the Other has rendered it unrecognizable. Absence has opened up a hole into which everything seems to fall. Breath fails us, and with it all of the natural ways in which our body usually responds. The one who has been abandoned is like a fish thrown from the water and forced to breathe in an environment that is no longer its own. The world as you knew it, the world that you inhabited before, the one brimming with a familiarity that was new every time, has turned to stone. It has withered, it is dead, it is burnt; it no longer exists as it did before. It is a closed world that does not welcome, but rejects. It is a world without a stage, uninhabitable, undesirable, inhospitable. The experience of abandonment lifts the surface of the meaning of the world, just as happens in an anatomy lesson when the nerves, bones and muscles of a corpse are exposed from beneath the skin. The image's casing gives way, it decomposes, it can no longer sustain the body, and the shapeless real of life appears in all its unfamiliar power. This is also why the world I once knew and lived in has now become entirely foreign. This is not simply a case of philosophy's astonishment when faced with the marvels of the world, but a traumatic emergence of the real that does not open the world but closes it. In abandonment we do not experience the opening of the world, but its closing. You are free, you can travel, walk, laugh, play, write, read, speak, but the meaning of travelling, walking, laughing, playing, writing, reading and speaking has failed. The world has fallen from its stage. Thus the world for those experiencing abandonment is a world that looks like the colourless world of the depressed.

4

The Work of Forgiveness

Courageous Love

Freud's judgement of love left no space for enchantment: according to him, falling in love has purely narcissistic roots. When we believe we love an other, in reality we always love ourselves, our ideal image that we see reflected in the one we love. Falling in love strengthens our I, exalting it and encouraging it to grow. To love is first and foremost to *love oneself*, to find in the other a mirror capable of highlighting our idealized traits. This is why Freud was suspicious of the Christian love for one's neighbour.[1] He believed that there is no altruism in human love, only the demand to narcissistically affirm our I through the other. From this, for example, comes his reading of the phenomenon of male jealousy, which he believed not to be in any way fed by the fear of losing a loved object, but by the projection onto the object of the strong urges to betray that unconsciously (or consciously) belong to him. Hence the inextricable relationship between love and hate: if I love the person I would like to be, insofar as I recognize the Other's autonomy and therefore their elusiveness, they also become an object of hate. As Lacan has taught us, idealization and aggression always travel together.[2]

We have seen, however, how love does exist that challenges the wisdom of this Freudian cynicism. It is a love that does not give precedence to the other reduced to an idealized mirror of the I, but gives it to the encounter with an exteriority that is loved for what it is, in its different and thorny real, and not because of the support it provides to my 'Ideal Ego'. This is love that respects distance, that feeds on the encounter with difference, that knows how to embrace the risky and absolute exposure to the Other with generosity and courage, beyond narcissism and repetition. It is a rare love, and Camus leaves us little hope when he says that such a love only occurs two or three times a century, and his was one of them.[3] But it does exist and often, as experience with analysis shows us. It is not the first love of a life but that which is reached only through other, less happy and sometimes traumatic experiences. Its foundation does not lie in any ideal Other, but in the contingency of the encounter that has made the experience of the Two possible and in the desire that this encounter may never finish, never run out, but repeat itself over and over.

This love is courageous because it is only possible if each of the Two knows how to accept their own destiny of being exiled from the existence of the sexual relationship. In this kind of love there is no isolation, no escape from the world, no search for an oblative fusion of One with the Other, but the new experience of the world made possible by knowing how to bear the weight of one's own solitude. This does not, however, mean that this love is safe from rupture, from the end of the trauma of betrayal or abandonment. Unlike narcissistic love, which lives in the symbiotic mirroring that cancels out all difference and transforms the bond into one of reinforced concrete or into furious, vengeful hate, it is sustained by the reciprocal solitude of the lovers and their free choice to be together rather than the forced need to exorcise the fear of loneliness. It is the love that has caused the world to be born in a new way, that has marked a life, generated passion capable of standing the test of time, children, family, responsibility, shared memories, experiences, interests, plans, pain, joy, eroticism and fatigue. It is a bond that is not worn out in the fleeting ecstasy of narcissistic falling in love, but that is capable of keeping the erotic bond intense and unique over time, dignifying the promise that unites all lovers: 'it will be forever!' It is a love that contradicts the cynical and scientific judgement of our time, according to which loving couples are fatally destined to boredom and the decay of desire.[4]

And yet, what happens in these bonds when one of the two betrays the other, when the promise fails, when there is another emotional experience cloaked in secret and deceit? What happens if the traitor then begs forgiveness? Are they asking to be loved again and, having declared that it is not like it used to be, now want everything to go back to how it was? In short, is it possible to forgive when the promise has been broken by the betrayal and deceit of a great love? Should we limit ourselves to repeating Freud's ruling that every love is a narcissistic dream, that neither the promise nor the love that lasts 'forever' exists? Should we spit on love and simply accept that the egoistic urge of the human being will eventually corrode it? Should we judge the promises of lovers and their vow of eternity to be a ridiculous illusion, a childish outburst of omnipotence, or madness even? Should we make fun of lovers in their attempts to make love last? Or should we try to face up to the experience of betrayal, with the offence caused by the person we love most, with the pain inflicted by the person who has always been a soothing figure? Should we not perhaps attempt to praise forgiveness in love? But what is forgiveness in love?

The Adulterous Woman

We are all familiar with the parable of the adulterous woman in the Gospel according to John (8:1–11). An unfaithful woman is dragged through the temple and thrown before Jesus, who is called upon with these words: 'Teacher, [. . .] this woman was caught in the act of adultery. The law of Moses says to stone her. What do you say?'

Jesus is crouching down. He writes something in the soil with his finger, the way children do. He is engrossed in what he is doing. He does not assume the upright position of the judge, of the one whose judgement will decide on absolution or condemnation. He does not want to judge anyone. Jesus does not underestimate the woman's guilt, but shifts the centre of the discourse from the imaginary dimension of guilt – as the outcome of an entirely formal and disciplinary relationship with the Law, and as an effect of the transgression of an external norm – to the symbolic guilt in relation to the betrayal of one's own desire. In other words, he shifts the centre of the discourse *from the exterior relationship of Law-desire to the relationship each*

person has with their own desire, with the Law of their own desire.
Are you so pure that you view yourselves as judges? Do you
have no relationship with desire? What do you know of the
Law of desire?

Jesus writes with his own finger, choosing a crouching position close to the earth. He does not pass sentence, he does not
judge, he does not absolve. He shows that he understands how
guilt can only be emended through the life freed by the Law,
and not through death sanctioned by the Law. No one can make
themselves the judge of another, no one has the right to decree
the death of another. He writes in the earth like a child absorbed
in his game. He does not want to take part in the dispute, despite
being dragged into it by those who would want to unmask
him as a false prophet, as a transgressor of Moses' law, which
unequivocally sanctions capital punishment for those who stain
themselves with the sin of adultery.[5]

By behaving in this way Jesus takes the side of the adulterous
woman. He stands by her side, he does not leave her on her
own as the husband and the lover do. The forgiveness that he
invokes for the woman is not meant as a gesture that falls from
on high. It should not be the result of a legalistic investigation
in which we ask, was this woman neglected by her husband?
Did she have good reason to betray him? Was the betrayal
a serious issue or an irrelevance? Rather than following the
legal logic of absolution or punishment, Jesus chooses the more
arduous road of forgiveness as an absolute gesture that is free,
radically autonomous. There cannot be forgiveness that does
not come from the earth, from our fall, that does not imply a

relationship between the person forgiving and their very being, or, as Lacan would say, their own division. Jesus' objection to the men in the Temple is the same as that put forward by the analyst to the 'beautiful soul' who insists on judging the situation without implicating themselves, without recognizing that they too play a part, that they have their own responsibility in the disorder they so resolutely condemn. Jesus is the only one in this scene who, as Françoise Dolto reminds us, is truly thinking of the woman, 'small hunted creature, paralysed by those men who have ripped her from her lover's bed'.[6] We all know the final words with which Jesus replies to the scribes and the Pharisees who invoke the merciless application of the Law of death, of punishment, without contemplating any possibility for redemption: 'He that is without sin among you, let him cast the first stone at her!' The pure judge the impure, exteriorizing onto them their own repressed or foreclosed impurity. This is the foundation for all extremism: the pure lay claim to their own integrity by refusing any contamination by the impurity of the Other, but what they omit (repress or foreclose) is that this impurity is actually a name for their very being, a name for the territory of the drive that constitutes them. This is why Jesus stays crouched on the floor, implicating himself in a movement of unique introjection of the Law that decrees the suspension of its sterilely universal character. The merciless application of the Law demanded by the Super-Ego (the Law of Moses) is deactivated, *suspended*.[7]

Jesus does not brandish the Law as if it were a stick, he does not judge ('I pass judgement on no one' (John 8:15)), but questions the unique relationship of each person with the Law of desire. The possibility for forgiveness is entirely contained in this movement of the Law's suspension and its subjective introjection: who am I, what allows my I to judge the Other, to condemn them without any possibility for release or redemption? Who am I to deny the Other another chance? Whilst the act of stoning implies a protective movement – the exteriorization of Evil, the paranoid identification of the guilty party in another – what Jesus invites us to do implies a symbolic movement of a return to oneself in order to gather the impurities of our own drives from the earth of our existence. It is for this reason that the act of forgiveness here contains no value judgement and must not be confused with the power of absolution. 'Neither do I condemn you', Jesus says to the woman before letting her go and before reminding her to 'leave your life of sin'. This invitation to 'leave your life of sin' is not a moralistic one. It would jar with the extra-moral tension that runs through the whole tale. 'Leave your life of sin' is said to remind the woman of the truth of her desire, the importance of recognizing that the Law that counts most, the one that counts more than the vengeful Law of retaliation, is the Law of one's own desire, the Law of love. Decide, choose, take control of your life, do not let yourself be trapped in an easy solution, do not renounce your freedom, do not confuse it with a passing fancy, live no longer in shadow and deceit! Rather than condemning, Jesus invites us to take responsibility for our own desire. He invites us to consider the existence of another Law beyond the universal one invoked by those who would see her stoned to death. This other Law is named by Lacan as the unique Law of desire.[8] It is no longer a case of formally opposing the Law *to* desire, but of presuming that desire is inhabited by a Law or, if you prefer, that desire itself is the only effective form of the Law. Indeed, desire must not be confused with passing fancy; it does not mean doing whatever you like, but taking on the dignity of a call, a vocation, a *Wunsch* (wish). Jesus invites the woman to follow her own desire, to leave ambiguity, to live her own life more coherently, not in the name of an external Law but in the name of the Law of her own desire.

To Forgive the Unforgivable?

Is then 'forgiving the unforgivable' – as Jacques Derrida puts it – not love's most radical gesture?

> In order to approach now the very concept of forgiveness, logic and common sense agree for once with the paradox: it is necessary, it seems to me, to begin from the fact that, yes, there is the unforgivable. Is this not, in truth, the only thing to forgive? The only thing that *calls* for forgiveness? If one is only prepared to forgive what appears to be forgivable, what the church calls 'venial sin', then the very idea of forgiveness would disappear.[9]

What we can forgive lies within the order of the excusable, of minor sin, something that has not damaged our existence, that has not shaken its very foundations. The betrayal of the promise, of the word of the promise, if it means betraying ourselves, if it indicates the failure of the call of desire and its Law, becomes truly unforgivable because it upends our entire existence. Lacan reminds us of this when he says that in every betrayal there is a point at which love can no longer be recovered, at which every possibility for redemption is lost.[10] It happens when the one we love insists on lying to themselves, when they insist on systematically betraying their own desire. So even the greatest love, the one given as an active, anti-narcissistic gift, does not limit itself to adoring the image of the other, but knows how to address the loved subject in their most detailed particularity, even if this love does not continue, even if it is interrupted or ends. This is the point at which forgiveness becomes truly impossible and love comes to a halt:

> There is a point at which it comes to a halt, a point which is only located in relation to being – when the loved being goes too far in his betrayal of himself and persists in self-deception, love can no longer follow.[11]

The unforgivable in love is not so much the hidden betrayal, but the betrayal of one's own desire, the subject's failure before their own Law. The most profound truth that psychoanalysis teaches us is, in fact, that the only betrayal is that of our own desire. For this reason, when a lover insists on fooling themselves, when they irreversibly distance themselves from their own desire, love, fatally, can no longer follow them.

Reflection by the Subject

The betrayal of the promise by the Other destroys trusting relationship that sustains love. The one who has been betrayed and does not want to fail the promise has two equally valid options: *to forgive the impossible or experience the impossibility of forgiveness*. Should we remain in the bond thanks to the forgiveness of the unforgivable, or accept the impossibility of forgiveness and experience the end of the bond?

Neither forgiveness nor the impossibility of forgiveness can, however, be the result of a conscious decision. This means that, in its most radical sense, both the act of forgiveness and the impossibility of forgiving never depend upon the other's behaviour but on a *reflection* made and a decision taken by the subject. The act of forgiveness exceeds any calculation by the object. It cannot depend on a fear of throwing a shared history of memories and desires to the wind, nor can it depend on an act of repentance by the one who has betrayed. Let us be clear: our forgiveness will never be made possible by something the Other has done. At the same time, we could say that the impossibility of forgiveness does not depend so much on a negative judgement of the one who has betrayed, but on the relationship between the one who has been betrayed and the (impossible) possibility of loving the other once more.

Forgiveness becomes truly possible when the subject who is forgiving has undergone a process affecting the most intimate parts of their life, so that any imagined symmetry with the offence is broken. But this takes time. Forgiveness is not a reactive act, but a *work* that takes time and that has as its essential premise the subject's reflection upon themselves. Faced with the total destruction of trust caused by the trauma of betrayal, only the work of forgiveness can renew *everything*, choosing the '*encore*' of love once more. As the very premise of forgiveness is to make a clear break with any symmetry or reciprocity, it can never take place as a result of behaviour by the one who has betrayed. Forgiveness is always asymmetric. It goes beyond the logic of exchange that stipulates one give to the Other only in order to receive something in return.[12]

In betrayal and abandonment we do not only experience the absence of the real of the Other, but also their most radical dis-idealization which imposes upon us (this is the main point I take from the Evangelical scene with the adulterous woman) a reckoning with our own real. The Other has revealed itself to be eccentric and dissonant with regard to every idealization, manifesting itself in the deceit and offence of the promise. We do not have to decide if this real face of the Other is worth our absolution (only God and judges decide to condemn or absolve), but if we are willing, with the love we still harbour, to renew our faith, to renew the gift of the promise. This is no simple task. But if our trust in the Other has been inevitably and irreversibly destroyed, it is only the subjective movement of the one who has been overrun by the trauma that can renew the pact. In this sense, the forgiveness is saying 'Yes!' – again 'Yes!' – to another possible encounter with the one we have loved. It is an absolute renewal of the bond that cannot pursue the illusion of rebuilding the bond exactly as it was.

Forgiveness cannot remove the marks of the wound, it cannot be the simple result of amnesia. Everything that surrounded the loved one – memories, experiences, children, friendships, endeavours – must be wanted a second time, must be made to live in a new way, again once more, *encore*. We can think of the act of forgiveness as one of the most noble acts of love. Only the work of forgiveness can make us decide on another 'Yes!', can prove despite it all that the face of the New truly is the face of the Same, can maintain the coincidence bound to its destiny.

The Impossibility of Forgiving Out Of Love

For narcissistic love, the work of forgiveness is impossible because the disappointment provoked by the Other generates such a wound in the I that the object can no longer exercise its ideal function of support. However, this is not the only version of the impossibility of forgiveness. When the impossibility of forgiveness does not come from a narcissistic offence, it can have the same dignity as forgiveness. Both experiences – forgiveness and the impossibility of it – can be in a close relationship with the impossible. The impossibility of forgiveness is no less important than a forgiveness that has taken place. The impossibility of forgiveness is not simply the failure of forgiveness. Even the impossibility of forgiveness can be a radical manifestation of love: an impossibility of accepting the deceit, the betrayal, the abandonment of the promise, not to defend an abstract Ideal, a purely platonic and idealizing version of love, or worse, of the image of our own I. It can be impossible to forgive because we do not want to shrink from the greatness of the encounter that we wanted to be forever. Something has broken and it defies all attempts to mend it. 'It's not like it used to be' is not just the sentence of the one who has abandoned and betrayed, or who quite simply no longer loves, but can also become the response of the one upon whom the wound of abandonment has been inflicted. It can also 'not be like it used to be' for those who have been subject to the trauma, as the shadow of infidelity, of the betrayal of the word, of deceit renders the Other untrustworthy, unrecognizable, foreign, different from the person with whom we had experienced the world in a new way.

The impossibility of forgiveness can be another way in which the absolute nature of love is made manifest, in relation to which forgiveness can seem like an easy route that would lead you to adapt to something (betrayal) that contradicts the very roots of this love. As such, every version of forgiveness in bad faith is rejected, because it is possible to forgive out of fear of losing the object, to preserve and defend the family, to avoid overly painful and time-consuming tears in our own lives. In each of these cases there has not been an effective work of forgiveness, but a *flight into forgiveness* (in the clinical sense with which Freud referred to a 'flight into illness') in order to avoid the anxiety-provoking encounter with our own loneliness and the loss of the loved object.[13]

The impossibility of forgiveness can be as great as forgiveness. The object that has wounded us is alive, it is still a presence but this presence has been corrupted, altered, transfigured, revealing itself to be different from what we believed it to be. In the impossibility of forgiveness this same presence becomes an absence, a non-being, a death that cannot be brought back to life. I decide that it is truly the end and that our lives no longer coincide. In this case, the work of forgiveness is replaced with the work of mourning: they are dead to me, they no longer exist, it is all over.

The possibility of forgiveness and the experience of forgiveness as impossible are not just two alternative options. Rather, they share a common point, they are two sides of the same coin. Both face the real hurdle of the impossible; love is, for them, a radical experience, a risk of absolute exposure to the Other. Of course, the impossibility of forgiveness opens life up to another path, one different from that of the work of forgiveness, confirming the irreversible death of the loved object. No starting over, no new beginning. The path of love has been irreversibly shattered. This option's proximity to the work of mourning is clearer. The object is lost, they are not really dead but are declared dead; they are no longer a part of my life. They have become an absolute absence and this loss without return must be symbolized. It is not and never will be like it used to be.

Forgiving the unforgivable and recognizing the impossibility of forgiving the unforgivable are two equally dignified ways of keeping faith in the absolute of love, of not being content with its ordinary degradation into the administration of a life without desire. The difference is that only the work of forgiveness can restart time and generate new joy. It does not dissolve everything that has been, but takes it forward, making it still possible in a new form. Conversely, the refusal to forgive proclaims the end by assuming the full consequences of the deceit. The lover remains faithful to their love as it was before the betrayal and it is because of this faithfulness that they are not willing to forgive. Is this an excess of idealism? Of neurotic fundamentalism? It is best not to judge the truth of love. I see the same greatness in refusing forgiveness out of love as I see in the work of forgiveness that allows us to forgive the unforgivable.

The Work of Forgiveness and the Work of Mourning

The work of forgiveness takes time: the memory of the offence is revisited over and over to the point where it reaches that oblivion which makes a new beginning possible. Could we say that this work has a similar nature to the Freudian work of mourning?[14] Is there a similarity between the work of mourning and that of forgiveness? It is most important to point out that these are not two reactions, but two labours. In order to be fully carried out, mourning and forgiveness *take time* (though is there a work of forgiveness or of mourning that is ever entirely 'finished'? One that leaves no residue, no scar left by the wound?). They are not consumed by the emotional and reactive response to pain, but are two symbolic processes that are upsetting and difficult given the real experience of loss. They both require an (unavoidable) work of memory. This means remembering someone who is no longer there, or who has interrupted their presence with the offence of betrayal. In the work of mourning, mental pain caused by the loss of the loved object provides a

84

location for the memory. Remembering how they were, what the world of the Two was like, what we were like and what we did together, what we have seen together. Remembering their objects: their glasses, their pipe, their hat, their walking stick, their books. The work of memory requires, as Freud reminds us, a 'certain lapse of time' that, by its very definition, excludes the possibility for a swift mourning period.[15] However, at the end of this long, painful mental process, the subject reaches a point of oblivion that can truly separate them symbolically from the lost object. In reference to this, Freud talks of a *libidinal disinvestment from the object*, which allows the libido to finally flow from the object that is no longer there, and which had been occupying it, so that it can once again direct itself towards other objects in the world. If, however, this disinvestment were not to happen, the subject would sink into the quicksand of melancholy, they would remain absolutely tied to the ever-present absence of the object, which would no longer be a lost object but one that is persecutory and impossible to forget. When a work of mourning is successful, the lost object is truly lost and allowed to go into the land of the dead. It has left us, we have suffered this loss, we can hold onto it symbolically *within ourselves*, but the world that has died with it can finally find another possible life, the world can take a new form.

The work of forgiveness in love also begins against the backdrop of an interruption of presence: the Other that we loved infinitely has turned their back on us, has betrayed their word, they have abandoned us. Their presence undergoes a traumatic eclipse, as we have seen. As when mourning, we find ourselves faced with a chasm that the Other has opened in the world and *within us*. And, as with the work of mourning, it is always *within us* (as shown by the crouching Christ in the scene with the adulterous woman) that the person who is no longer with us must be symbolized. Because it is always and only *within us* that we experience the lack of the Other.[16]

In this profound sense, the work of forgiveness is intertwined with the work of mourning. In mourning, as in forgiveness, the subject faces up to the non-response of the Other. In mourning this is because the Other is dead, they are no longer there, they have left us and any attempt to bring back their presence is destined to fail miserably. 'There is no answer. Only the locked door, the iron curtain, the vacuum, absolute zero.'[17] Mourning is obliged to recognize, as Derrida would say, that the difference between the One and the Other is linked to the fact that one leaves forever *first*, leaving the other with memory and loneliness,[18] forcing upon them a reckoning with a real absence that requires the re-signification of the entire world, given that '[t]he act of living is different all through. Her absence is like the sky, spread over everything.'[19]

In forgiveness, the reckoning with the non-response of the Other assumes different forms because, unlike that which happens in the case of mourning, the absence of the Other generates, for the one who is still in love, a presence at the very limit of the persecution that extends like a shadow over the subject's life, as Freud would say.[20] The object of forgiveness is not eclipsed in an irreversible way, *they are not a dead object*. Whilst with mourning there is nothing left of the object – they really have

86

gone to the land of the dead – the work of forgiveness is confronted with the interruption of the presence without the loss of the object being irreversible. The subject of forgiveness is faced with the subject of the offence who is still alive, who has not stopped living in any way. Particularly in cases where they are still there and *asking* for forgiveness: they want to be forgiven, they want to restart the loving discourse that they themselves have interrupted. It is therefore the subject that must decide whether or not to give life to that love once more, or to declare its definitive end. It is the subject that must decide whether to let the Other go in their absence or whether to recall their presence: I am the one who must decide if their image must die or not.[21] If with real mourning we face the impossibility of life in the face of death, with forgiveness we face the possibility of saving the Other from death. The Other is still there, present, alive. They ask in different ways to be forgiven, they ask that we not destroy everything as they themselves had tried to do, that they be given what they have not given: the recovery of the truth of the promise. On the one hand therefore, given the betrayal and deceit, the Other is dead, but on the other, they still exist and are calling not for an absolution that does not exist, but our forgiveness. Therefore *they are dead and alive at the same time*. They are totally absent and totally present. And it is precisely this strange presence of the object – off-kilter, ruined, topsy-turvy – that clearly differentiates the work of mourning from that of forgiveness. It is as if forgiveness faces us with both a wound to be mourned – the object is lost, it is not like it used to be – and also the possibility of a new beginning, of its resurrection.

But will the word of the one I loved and who has betrayed me ever find its value again? Will the Other ever again be able to gain my trust? The work of forgiveness rotates around a point of dissonance and absence to which the ideal Other has retreated. We have already seen this: this hole that has opened in the Other is a name of the Other's difference from the ideal Other, it is a name of the most real real of the Other. It is a deviation by the Other that no operation of symbolization will ever be able to reabsorb. With forgiveness, the offence endured will not be cancelled out, but will leave a trace, a wound, a scar. However, in one case – that of mourning – there is an *excess of absence*, whilst in the other – that of forgiveness – there is an *excess of presence*. For both of these a point of oblivion must be reached through memory. Otherwise, as we have seen, remembering the loss of the dead, or the wound of betrayal and abandonment, can become a melancholic rumination. The fixation on the memory of the trauma must be able to provide breathing space; it must embrace the plasticity of the drive so that forgiveness, when its work is done, can become a vital form of oblivion.

Forgiveness and Gratitude

The work of forgiveness recognizes the otherness of the Other as something that cannot be assimilated to our own identity. It revolves around its irreducible freedom, it recognizes the crease that cannot be smoothed, the wrinkling, the puckering of the Other's wall, the distance that separates the real of the loved object from every possible ideal representation. The interruption of the loved one's presence pushes the subject once more towards the black of night, like the first blow for the torture victim as told by Jean Améry. This is why forgiveness is work that can only be carried out in solitude: to grasp the body of the now-estranged Other with uncertainty, as if blind, in order to finally be able to recognize their identity once more. This movement towards the night offers the chance to cross through the narcissistic bubble of our ideal image, to extract ourselves from absolute abandonment once more.

The work of forgiveness can become – as it sometimes does – an opportunity to attempt to take a step beyond the quicksand of narcissism. The pride of the I tends to make this work impossible, rejecting the violence of the offence, but it is for precisely this reason that there is nothing like the experience of forgiveness – when it truly happens – to show the limitations of the Freudian view of love as blinding, as pure imaginary illusion. The Other here is not a good mirror that reflects the best parts of me, offering a libidinal restocking that enriches my narcissism, nor are they reduced, as when they go, to a smashed mirror that cannot give anything back and that becomes the object of hate and repulsion. Falling in love as 'mental lust', according to a definition by Lacan that binds us to the illusory and persecutory traits of the mirror, makes way for another love.[22] The work of forgiveness is not fed by narcissistic infatuation with one's own ideal image, but comes from the abyss of the trauma of abandonment. It does not confront the subject with the ideal image of the Other, but its most thorny otherness, with the most real real of the Other. If falling in love is satisfied with the strengthening of the I, forgiveness leads beyond it, bringing us closer to the mystery of the total recalcitrance of the Other, of its being irreducibly foreign, *heteros*.

However, the word 'forgiveness' has never had any currency in psychoanalysis. Perhaps the closest concept is that of 'gratitude' found in Melanie Klein's lexicon.[23] What does gratitude refer to? In Klein's terms, the child comes into the world devoured by primitive anxieties about death provoked by the fact that they cannot control their own body, the excess of life that runs through them and the chaos that impregnates them. The child is surrounded by the excessive drives of life without being able to escape them or find shelter from them. The *ruthless love* that Winnicott believed characterized the child's primary sadistic-oral relationship with the mother's body, reduced to a partial object, is a blind urge towards the appropriation that strays into destruction of the self and the Other. Faced with the anxiety of death that submerges the child, they attack the object filled with aggression in order to appropriate it and deny its otherness.[24] The breast is denied as an external, independent object and is fantasmatically incorporated, and therefore destroyed in its otherness. The unlimited voracity of the oral drive, however, rebounds against the subject in the form of a persecutory view of the outside world: the more intense the aggression unleashed from it towards the object, the more threateningly the object will assail the subject. The only Law that is at work here is the imaginary one of retaliation – an eye for an eye, a tooth for a tooth – which excludes the mediation of forgiveness. There is, in fact, a directly proportionate nexus between the sadism of the Super-Ego and the intensity of the destructive aggression aimed at the Other, which allows no symbolic mediation. Klein refers to this negative cycle, in which the aggressive urge generated by the anxiety of death is repeated in the subject as a feeling of persecution and hostility and a destructive aversion to the world, as 'paranoid-schizoid'. It is the thesis she fully develops in *Envy and Gratitude*, in which the pole of envy unites within it the most archaic paranoid-schizoid fantasies, marking a solely destructive relationship with the object that is rich in enjoyment, but leaves the subject alone when faced with their anxieties about death.

Unlike envy, gratitude springs from the recognition of the damage inflicted upon the object of love, which has been mercilessly attacked because of their otherness and autonomy. When faced with the threat of the object hurt by envy and filled with bitter resentment, paranoid-schizoid anxiety transforms into a new fear, no longer caused by the persecutory violence *of* the object, but *for* the object, as having been able to wound, damage, destroy. This means that gratitude is able to recognize the symbolic debt owed to the Other and warmly welcomes the rediscovery of the object in its otherness. Whilst with persecutory anxiety the subject is attacked by the object, fearing its retaliation, in depressive anxiety, from which gratitude comes, the subject is positively mobilized *towards* the object. It recognizes what it has received from the object and everything it owes to it. In this sense, the emergence of feelings of gratitude towards the Other signals the end of jealous hatred and the possibility of a new beginning. We see this very regularly in psychoanalysis. When the clouds of envy begin to clear, a new feeling of gratitude can spring forth (in Lacanian terms gratitude is simply the recognition of our provenance from the Other, of the gift received from language, of the gift of life and the word that comes from the Other).

Why Men Find It More Difficult to Forgive

Being cheated on does not do wonders for our Ego. The anthropological figure of the cuckold carries the stigmata of humiliation. Forgiveness does not earn us any prestige, because it always assumes (as far as possible) a distancing from one's own narcissistic image. This is why men find it more difficult to forgive. Their attachment to the Ego is stronger, more cumbersome than in women as it is sustained by the presence – imaginary (virile competition) and real (presence of the organ) – of the phallus. Indeed, Lacan spoke of a phallic encumbrance that dulls the life of men, making them more sensitive than women to the narcissistic value of the importance of their image.[25] Whilst a woman tends to relativize her own identity, to be more open to exchange with, contamination by and a relationship with the Other, to experience her own image not as a rigid identity but as a form open to transformation, a man tends to view his identity as a uniform. And when this (entirely phallic) identity finds itself in crisis – as happens, for example, with betrayal – the most normal reaction is the indignant and furious rejection of the person who has cheated, to the (detestable though not uncommon) point of violence. For a man, seeing himself cheated on by a female partner leads to an encounter with the depths of his own castration, with his own phallic devaluation, with his own lack of being, with a real unravelling of his own identity. For a man, recognizing the freedom of the Other – which is also freedom of error and betrayal – moves in the opposite direction to that phallic passion *of having* that usually drives his life. The Other's freedom throws into crisis his fantasy of appropriation, demonstrating the limit of his own phallic power and consequently forcing him to face up to the open wound of castration. And for a man to make contact with his own castration is much more difficult, more arduous, more traumatic than for a woman, for whom castration belongs (as it were) to the very structure of her being. For this reason, phallic pride usually opposes the work of forgiveness, throwing up a barrier against the recognition of his own vulnerability. Forgiveness is replaced by the demand for justice (as happens with the group of men watching the scene of the adulterous woman), if not blind violence or simply the furious refusal of the Other.

Violence Without Law

There was a time in which the Law of Codes authorized brutal male violence in the face of the dishonour of betrayal, without the opposite being true for women. It was a discrimination that justified and ideologically supported that violence. Women were considered an object in men's hands, to do with as they wished. The right to ownership of women by men was fatally combined with legal rulings. Male violence including crimes of passion were justified by a need to re-establish the honour and superiority of man over woman. Today, things have changed. Just feminist demands have emancipated women from this position of an object subject to the male will, and the legal Codes have progressively had to adapt to this new cultural climate. However, precisely as women's voices have begun to gather strength, starting to be raised more decisively than ever, the cases of femicide and violence against women perpetrated by men have multiplied. It is thought that at least one woman out of three worldwide has been on the receiving end of violence perpetrated by men.

Violence is always a blunt alternative to the Law of the word. Conversely, there is nothing closer to that Law than the work of forgiveness. Violence can be a reaction to the betrayal of a promise: if the Other has denied the truth of the pact, violence claims the right to brutally deny the existence of the Other. It is a kind of pure retaliation deprived of any symbolic mediation and driven by a need for revenge. It particularly happens in narcissistic love, in which the idealization of the image of the Other always implies an unconscious aggression towards it: I love you because you represent my Ideal Ego, but as I cannot be you, as I cannot coincide in you, I hate you to death.

The drive to blind violence, to subjugation, to envious hate, to the destruction of the Other, is not a pathology but has always accompanied human history like a shadow. It is no coincidence that the Old Testament finds one of its first and most disturbing figures in the atrocious and unjustifiable act of Cain. We must not close our eyes to this uncomfortable truth: the killing of one's brother out of jealousy is not an act that belongs to the animal kingdom but exclusively to the human one. It is one – terrifying – aspect of the human being that we cannot misrecognize by attributing it to the animal kingdom or, worse still, to a human regression to an animal state. The crime is not a sign of this regression, as a bad moralistic culture would have us believe, but expresses a truly human tendency. This is the thesis forcefully declared by the young Lacan, dissociating the crime from a presumed regression of man to the brutality of animal instinct:

> [It is] that man's ferocity towards his semblable exceeds every-thing animals are capable of, and that carnivores themselves recoil in horror at the threat man poses to nature as a whole.[26]

Violence and Love

The spread of violence in our world is heightened by a culture that imposes a vision of humans as an enjoyment machine programmed for their own self-affirmation. When something contradicts this end, violence comes into play as a powerful tool with which to remove any obstacle. Conversely, the humanization of life always occurs as a problematic reckoning with the violence within us – lurking in our darkest shadows – in order to arrive at the possibility of its rejection in the name of the Law of the word. This is one of the most difficult tasks facing human beings: *knowing how to renounce violence in the name of the recognition of the Other as our neighbour, as a unique being, as absolute difference.* It is a recognition that is never without pain because it obliges us to accept that 'I am not everything', that the life of the world and those of others are not entirely consumed by my own. It means putting up with what Freud considered to be a 'narcissistic blow' necessary for recognizing ourselves as belonging to a human Community.[27]

For psychoanalysis, violence is never entirely removed from love.[28] It does not accept the cliché that love views violence as pure sacrilege, and as such, excludes it outright. Contesting this thesis, we have the love stories of men and women that appear to be regularly afflicted by a violence that seems to be unleashed by loving passion rather than being its direct opposite. Why do certain women choose men *not despite the fact they are violent but precisely because they are*? Let us reconsider the dramatic and paradigmatic case of Rosaria Aprea, an aspiring Miss Caserta who was beaten almost to death by her boyfriend. It was not the first time, since Rosaria had already been beaten during that relationship. But the most disconcerting thing is that in hospital she declared that her greatest desire was to return to the man who had persecuted her! In this and many other cases, the encounter with the violence of the Other does not activate a normal reaction of flight but bafflingly demands its repetition. This is the scandal: *encore*, again, more beatings, more gratuitous violence, more humiliation! In another girl's case, that of sixteen-year-old Fabiana, we see repetition to the point of death: she ends up being burned alive by her boyfriend. For one of my patients who had reported her partner numerous times for battery, the problem was not the abuse to which she was subjected, but not being able to live apart from him. She realized that the relationship humiliated her and was leading her to ruin but she could not do without it. Is this feminine masochism? Why do many women choose the worst for their love lives? Why do they throw themselves into the arms of men who treat them only as objects? For many women, the difficulty of subjectivizing their otherness – the difficulty of being women – is falsely resolved by throwing themselves into the arms of men who offer the illusion of being compasses capable of guiding their path before transforming themselves into predatory tyrants.[29]

This is not simply a case of good cultural education. Following Freud's teaching, we must remember that human beings are not merely guided by the pleasure principle; they do not pursue their own well-being avoiding anything that might bring them displeasure. The great, subversive contribution made to human philosophy by psychoanalysis is to demonstrate how human beings have a tendency – what was referred to by Freud as being 'beyond the pleasure principle' – to search out the very thing that does them most harm, the repetition of something that has traumatically unbalanced the homeostatic equilibrium of the pleasure principle. In other words, when faced with what does them most harm, human beings do not naturally move away from it as quickly as possible, but adopt the paradoxical stance that pushes them to immerse themselves in it fully.[30]

This emerges clearly in the case of Lucia, a teacher whose knowledge of women's rights was strongly politicized. In her most intimate self she carried with her the shadow of a violent man from whom she was unable and, deep down, did not *want* to separate. From her family story featuring a perennially depressed mother, there emerged a heavily idealized, Oedipal falling-in-love with the father who, however, from the point of adolescence, suddenly (and phobically) distanced himself from the girl who had, up until that point, been his favourite daughter. He began ridiculing her for her difficulties with schoolwork and then the beatings started. The father of love traumatically revealed himself to be the father of disdain and abuse. Lucia placed excessive importance on beauty in order to compensate for her feeling of having no value whatsoever. And so she began to collect disastrous love stories that were all characterized by men who used her body without giving her the love she searched for. The traumatic encounter with her father's duplicity repeated itself relentlessly: to be insulted, depraved, raped each time. Lucia was willing to do anything to avoid losing her father's love.[31]

The Tender Assassin

Last spring I was invited to take part in a meeting with inmates at the Opera jail, a maximum-security prison in Milan. It was the first time in my life I had set foot in a prison, the first time I had entered a place where freedom was not just limited by an institutional framework (as with a school or hospital) but in which it was systematically and materially denied. I immediately felt this exclusion in all of its harshness, and continued to do so until the end of my visit. The inmates stained by the most serious crimes had dedicated part of their time to studying my book *Ritratti del desiderio* [*Portraits of Desire*], studying the word 'desire' in its various declensions.[32] I had accepted this invitation because it seemed to me an extraordinary opportunity to dedicate a reading workshop to the word 'desire' without having material access to freedom! At the end of our conversation, a number of inmates sat next to me and showed me their reflections and read me some poetry. I was struck in particular by a young man who was not much over twenty, with a strong Calabrian accent, handsome and well-built, with clear, deep, dark eyes, well-dressed and capable of intelligently discussing complex themes such as those we had attempted to talk about as a group. He objected to Lacan's idea that desire tends to move itself infinitely from one object to the next without stopping, without ever finding its adequate fulfilment. This representation of desire seemed unacceptable to him because it excluded the unique and irreplaceable character of the object of love. 'Can't an object exist', he rightly asked, 'that doesn't allow itself to be overwhelmed by the insatiable metonymy of desire? Can't there be an absolute love capable of stopping the mindless motion of desire?'

Saying goodbye to them, I was curious and asked the friend who had invited me about the nature of the crime committed by that boy whose sensitivity and mildness had struck me. Her response stopped me in my tracks, sending a chill down my spine: 'He strangled his girlfriend out of jealousy', she told me. He was a killer. That boy who tried to defend the irreplaceability of the object of love, the boy with all that tenderness in his eyes was a killer! Why had he done it? Why had he ruined his own life and decreed the death of his partner with an unacceptable act of violence? Out of 'absolute love?', I thought sadly to myself. It immediately seemed, however, too easy to throw scorn on that act or, more precisely, exclude it disdainfully from the realms of human possibility in love. It was far too easy to say: 'No! Absolute love is something else, this has nothing to do with it, this is something entirely different!' It was just as easy as insisting on the total difference between love and violence. It is true, of course, we all know this: absolute love as love for a woman or a man – as love for the *heteros* – *excludes violence out of principle* because violence is the most detestable manifestation of the absence of respect for the Other's existence. We can, therefore, immediately chase this image as a violent profanation of love as far from ourselves as possible without any fear of being wrong. It is true; this is exactly the case! And yet, in the monstrous contradiction between the loving ideal and the passage to the homicidal act, in the desperate sweetness of that gaze that I cannot forget, in that guilty and absurd way of realizing the promise of 'forever', I could not help but see a truth that tried to express itself, albeit in an entirely unacceptable and unjustifiable way. In the face and the words of that young man I didn't just see the wicked and bloody profanation of love. I also saw the power of love that had (guiltily) not found the right path to realization, manifesting itself solely as mortal hatred, wicked destruction, an incapacity to welcome the hard kernel of the Other's freedom. In the words that he tried to use to articulate his thoughtful objection to Lacan, that young man attempted to defend a version, albeit insane and fundamentalist, of absolute love in the face of the nihilist cynicism that renders all objects in the world equal. In this way, he dared touch the centre of his personal drama, as well as the tragic contradiction that accompanies all human love: the contradiction between the urge to appropriate and the respect for the Other's otherness.

In the case of this killer with kind eyes, his idealized vision of love ended up monstrously confusing itself with the executioner's right to arbitrarily decide on the death of his victim. And yet, I still had the indelible impression that in this contrast, at the very limits of what is bearable, something of the truth of human love was made manifest. Absolute love was associated in a disturbing way with the savage and unjustifiable violence of murder. But, I asked myself when I finally left the prison and could once more breathe in the spring air that was arriving in Milan, does human love not always contain, even latently, the contrast between our finite existence and the urge to the infinite of absolute love? Is it not always human love that is one step from crossing into violence? How can we infinitely love the Other without crossing the boundaries of their freedom? Is that human disease of jealousy that is far too human, sometimes very close to delirium, not perhaps an effect, at times farcical, at times tragic, of this contrast? Does the jealous lover project their fantasies of unfaithfulness onto the other or fear that distant wounds of abandonment will be repeated, that someone will take away the exclusive object of their love? Do they want to betray or do they fear they will lose once more that which they have already lost once? When it becomes pathological, does jealousy not perhaps indicate the thrilling bond between the urge to appropriate that can drive loving passion and violence in a distorted way?[33]

Absolute Exposure to Love

The contrast between freedom and ownership dramatically comes to light in the sweet eyes of the murderer in the Opera prison. Those eyes stayed with me for days. That young man had known love and in his jealousy-fuelled delirium he had killed it, in the name of love. Is this not what happens in all fundamentalism? Does killing in the name of God not carry with it the same tragic paradox? Every time we introduce the term 'absolute' we must always expect a fall into the insane mirages of totality. But this is not the sense in which I propose it in this book. Absolute love is such because it does not pursue fusion with the Other, it does not demand its appropriation but is ready to renounce all claims of ownership. It is only absolute insofar as it exposes itself absolutely to the freedom of the Other, without reservation, without delay and without hesitation. Conversely, the absolute love of the young killer was driven by a predatory fantasy which transfigured that love, changing it into a crazed and homicidal passion. This guiltily forgets that to love is *an absolute risk that excludes absolute possession* although, as we have seen, in love there is an urge to want to possess the loved object absolutely.

This contrast between possession and freedom inhabits every love life with no possibility of resolution. The psychoanalyst is well aware that the human experience of love is always an experience of encroachment. This is why jealous fantasies regularly accompany loving desire in both women and men, whilst jealous frenzies or fantasies do not exist in the animal kingdom. Jealousy remains an exquisitely human sentiment: the anxiety of being replaced, that someone else might take our place, that they might intrude on the exclusive intimacy of the Two, the anxiety of losing love, that the Other might find someone who cancels out our value for them, who takes our place in their desire. The point is that there is always something in human love that concerns excess, the failure of boundaries, the loss of the right measure. It is this excess that can lead a young man with kind eyes and a calm disposition to strangle an innocent woman. We scream out against the unforgivable crime of femicide and we add that there is nothing more horrible than a murder committed in the name of love! Nothing is more scandalous, nothing could be further from love! And yet, in this atrocious scene there is something that requires a more critical reflection. At the risk of seeming blasphemous we can evoke the figure of Saint Francis. Is Francis' love for Jesus not excessive, immoderate, unrestrained? Is it not a passion that overwhelms the Aristotelian virtue of the right measure, of the wise and prudent avoidance of extremes? Is this encounter not the encounter with a real? What leads him to squander his family's wealth, to rid himself of it all, to get rid of his own inheritance, to leave everything, lose everything, to jump into the void? Is this love shown by Francis for his God not 'mad'? Of course, Francis does not kill anyone for love, he is not in any way violent, he does not exercise any control over the Other. And yet, his love exudes excess. Should we not then contemplate a crazy dimension in every human love worthy of this name? When a man and a woman are *gripped* by love are they not always, do they not always seem a bit mad? Love always implies the experience of overcoming a limit, crossing a threshold, expending oneself. It is not just a *rediscovery of the self* as the harmonious metaphor proposed by Plato through Aristophanes in the *Symposium* would have us believe, but a *losing oneself*, an *exposing oneself absolutely, without reservation, to the unknown of the Other's desire*.[34] For this reason true freedom is not, as neurosis believes, an avoidance of a bond with the Other, an affirming of our autonomy, but it is knowing how to recognize our inadequacy and dependence on the Other. It does not consist of living without the Other because this is the profoundly narcissistic and perverse dream of every neurotic. Rather, true freedom implies the bond with the Other as that which opens my life to the ungovernable unknown of desire. Invoking freedom as a realization of oneself as an alternative to any bond instead results only in an entirely sterile fantasy of self-consistency. Cancelling out the symbolic dependence on the Other does not make life independent but mutilates it, walling it up on itself, reducing it to an empty fortress. This is what many neurotics do not want to see: staying alone is not, they often complain, a source of suffering, but their unconscious way of avoiding the anxiety-provoking danger of the absolute exposure to the Other's desire imposed by every loving encounter.

Virgil's Gloves

In the psychoanalytic treatment of obsessive neurosis, we often find at the forefront the subject's anguished refusal of the risk that this absolute exposure to the Other's desire carries with it. The administration of assets, keeping one's own property in a safe, the duplication of objects (wife and lover) are needed by many obsessives in order to avoid fully experiencing that leap into the void that the loving encounter demands. The choice for the Same promotes a repetition, not in the name of desire but in the name of a phobic forestalling of an urge to cheat or the routine regulation of one's own emotional life. This administrative version of love is not a form of love but its bureaucratic negation. This is the case with Virgil, the prominent antiques auctioneer and protagonist of *The Best Offer* by Giuseppe Tornatore (2013), whose passion for gloves and paintings keep him separate, maintaining a safe distance from the real of the encounter with the Other sex and the incontrollable combustion of love. Even his name carries an ideal of purity and lack of contamination that preserves the subject's very being. The glove as a form of non-contact, of artificial mediation, of avoidance of the encounter with the Other's hands, and the portraits of female faces that fill a secret room in his house – access to which is forbidden to all – realize the fantasy of having contact with the Other sex without ever doing so, without ever truly exposing himself to the risk it brings.

The film's surprise conclusion – which sees Virgil conned by a woman with whom he had fallen wildly in love, and her young friend, who steal all of those portraits jealously held in his secret room, the result of his life's work – demonstrates all of the risks implied by absolute exposure to love, particularly for those men for whom, as we have seen, such exposure appears to go against their phallic nature because it implies a loss, a concession of what one has, a lack that cannot be governed. For Molière's miser or for Verga's Mastro Don Gesualdo there is nothing more anxiety-provoking than the possibility of losing one's own things! This is why they will never make that step taken by Virgil, wanting instead to always keep themselves beyond the absolute risk of love. For Virgil, the abyss of depression opens up when, finally convinced of wanting to expose himself to love, he abandons his passion for dead objects and entrusts himself to the woman who has provoked his desire, awakening it from the torpor of an aridly isolated life. Except that, once he is mercilessly robbed of everything, he realizes that at least those dead objects guaranteed him this impersonal identity that love has irrevocably taken from him. We know that the loving encounter does not render life more harmonious, nor does it regulate its rhythms in a prudent and ordered way. The euphoria that accompanies the loving encounter is an indicator of an excess that unbalances, destabilizes, that drags away. In this sense, love is never an experience of mastery. On the contrary: *we do not possess love, but are possessed by it*. It moves, transports, leads us elsewhere. Rather than the reconstruction of a lost original balance as per Plato's illusory hypothesis, love always implies a break with equilibrium, particularly by its spontaneity. The contingency of the loving encounter exposes us without any guarantee, without any insurance: the breaking of equilibriums which it can provoke, to the point of total diso-rientation, is not a strengthening of the I and its narcissism, or rather, it is not only this. Rather, it signals the disappearance of the I, the loss of its mastery, its absolute exposure to that which it cannot demand to govern from above. This confusion can generate anxiety. It is the reason why obsessives always keep themselves at a certain distance from the contingent possibility of the loving encounter, as Virgil's immense glove collection sadly signals.[35]

Narcissism and Depression

Violence towards oneself or an other frequently takes the place of a failure to symbolize one's own lack. It happens between parents and children when the latter's violence can be unleashed by the bitter realization of having renounced their own life in order to meet – in a deep deception – their parents' expecta-tions.[36] It also happens between men and women when one of the two cannot bear the distancing of the Other, feeling themselves authorized to react violently in order to re-establish the authority of their own narcissistic image which has been sullied and humiliated. There is no other psychological reason for femicide, though there are other, profound cultural motives:

to use violence, the passage to the brutal act instead of assuming the burden of one's own solitude and one's own failure. Love as absolute exposure to the Other's desire is not what is at play here, but an explosive mixture of narcissism and depression. In the background is what Pasolini would have defined a real 'anthropological mutation': the hyper-modern man becomes a headless machine of enjoyment.[37] And when this machine functions less well, when it is not sufficiently oiled, has run out of fuel or, more simply, it breaks and loses efficiency, the fall into the void becomes fatal. This is why the current epidemic spread of depression can only be understood against this backdrop of anthropological mutation. It is no longer a depression that stems from the 'philosophical' and existential experience of the void and the senselessness of existence (just think of the paradigmatic meditations by Leopardi and Schopenhauer) but one that is generated by a defect in adapting to the imperative of the New and individual Success. Anyone left behind is cut out, whoever does not participate in this 'total mobilization' of life towards its positive affirmation experiences life as superfluous, insignificant, useless to society, and falls into the depths of depression. We must not forget how the diagnosis of depression is reached for every time we find ourselves faced with acts of unjustifiable violence. It is not an alibi, quite the contrary. It is no coincidence that Lacan scandalously insisted depression was a '*faute morale*' or a *moral failing*.[38] This is a thesis that is not entirely removed from the judgement the Fathers of the Church passed on sloth, and its aim is to demonstrate how in depression the subject always has a responsibility that must not be forgotten. This coincides with the difficulty of symbolically assuming one's own failure, one's own lack of success, the narcissistic wound inflicted on one's own image. If I am not the I that I believed myself to be (narcissism), it no longer makes sense to exist (depression). This is why the victim's murder is often followed by the assassin's suicide. Faced with a culture that seems to reject the formative value of failure and that teaches the mirages of the New and individual Success, resorting to violence can seem like a maleficent talisman with which to exorcise the fatal reckoning with our own inadequacy from which new flowers could grow.

Woman's Foreign Language

In love there is not a blinding, but admiration. That which Freud names as the narcissistic overestimation of the object only provides an effective portrayal of the loving scene in its first moments. The admiration of love goes well beyond the illusion of idealization. What is admired in the Other breaks the imaginary specularity in which One sees only their idealized representation in the Other. What is admired in love is the freedom of the Other, their maximum exteriority to ourselves, their being truly Other, non-identical to the One of my enjoyment. For this reason, admiration of love can never be an appropriation as it is actually the condition of every authentic learning experience. The same thing happens with foreign languages. Experience tells us that you learn them much more quickly if you love the person who is teaching them. The same thing could be said of any form of knowledge. In love it is the Other's desire that drags us on. It is their way of touching, feeling, looking, of experiencing the world that moves us and sets us in motion. In this sense, love, when it exists, is a pure admiration for the Other's desire. As a result, to love means to allow the Other to live their own desire to its fullest degree and with total freedom. There is no love – unless it is pathological and narcissistic – that is detached from this esteem. To admire the Other remains the most particular condition of love, one that cannot be reduced to the imaginary and protective strategies of identification.

The jealousy towards the Other's life that often afflicts neurotic subjects – jealousy, like love, does not have as its object a quality of the Other, but is pure 'Lebensneid',[39] a jealousy of the Other's life – is replaced by the astonished contemplation of that life. For this reason, Freud rightly noted how many patients often fluctuate between feelings of love and hate. Jealousy and admiration are indeed two very closely linked emotions. But whilst in envy the jealous party experiences the free and vivacious existence of the Other as a source of pain, in admiration this same existence causes satisfaction and increases desire. The subject that loves does not harbour envy for the existence and the affirmative power of the person they love, because they know how to enjoy it fully. Love is not just the love of the Other's castration and inadequacy. It is also the possibility of enjoying their generative force, their spontaneity, their full existence. This also happens during sex: the fullness of the Other's orgasm is not indifferent to my enjoyment, rather it strengthens it, expands and enriches it. At play here is not a sense of appropriation of the idealizing identification of narcissistic love, but a learning of the Other's foreign language. Violence refuses love even though it can manifest itself in the name of love, as we have seen happen in the throes of jealousy. In men, it is not just the thorny manifestation of power, perpetuated by a patriarchal culture that has historically discriminated against women, but, as clinical experience shows us, it is above all the expression of a profound anxiety felt by many men in the face of the indecipherable lexicon of love. Freud had already suggested this, in his own way, when he spoke of the 'repudiation of femininity', the boldest expression of neurosis described as not just affecting men, but also women.[40] Something about the 'here be dragons' of femininity provokes anxiety, is rejected, causes a refusal by both sexes. It is that dimension that is not entirely identifiable, measurable, governable, which accompanies the radical anarchy of the feminine being. The refusal of the feminine particularly affects men, who have built an entire Civilization – patriarchy – on this very refusal. The woman is a foreign language for every man, one that demands a continuous and never complete effort to learn, because this language cannot be codified. There is no dictionary capable of cataloguing its meaning. We do not even know the letters that make up its alphabet. Hence Lacan's affirmation that *love is always heterosexual* in the sense that there is always 'love for women', for the *heteros* that a woman knows how to embody. The reference here is not to heterosexuality as a simple anatomical difference between the sexes, but of the very condition of *heteros*, and its presence as an ineliminable condition of every loving discourse, be it a heterosexual or homosexual relationship.[41]

The violence visited upon the body and mind of women is a way of refusing this lesson, to circumvent the hard kernel of this alphabet, to force women to speak the only language known to men – the phallic one. The encounter with the woman always implies a quota/level of anxiety for *every* man, even if it is arrogantly misrecognized – the very thing needed by the group with which he can barbarically share the violence. The foreign language of the feminine – the radical *heteros* that it embodies – can never be fully assimilated. This can cause male violence to take on the most hateful and vicious forms, as if in the fatal vendetta, in the disfigurement, abuse, killing and burning of the female body, the alphabet of love and the effort that this requires could be destroyed forever.

'They Are All Whores!'

Without resorting to explicit violence, an obsessive man who suffered from premature ejaculation had turned this symptom into a sort of sadistic tool with which to strike his partner's desire, which was clearly a source of anxiety for him. During sex, the woman had to stay perfectly still because the slightest movement would have caused him to ejaculate, incapable as he was of controlling his urge to enjoy. This led to the real mortification of his partner's body, which had to stay silent and as immobile as a rock. This man, profoundly anxiety-ridden by the otherness of the feminine sex, had conjured up this system in an attempt to circumvent the alphabet of love and dominate the woman's body, making her dead, a lifeless mummy, an object at his service entirely deprived of her own freedom. This was the unconscious advantage that governed his symptom. This does not exempt us, as analysts, from also questioning his partner's desire: why did she accept being with a man who wanted her as if dead, made of stone, deprived of freedom?[42]

The refusal to learn the foreign language of woman demonstrates how male violence towards women has always been without culture in its profound sense. This violence is not solely meted out by poor, uneducated subjects; even rich, powerful and intelligent men can violate women. The absence of culture consists of the stubborn refusal to learn the alphabet of love. The foreign language of woman can cause men to fall in love or grow wild with rage. 'They are all whores!' then becomes the misogynist mantra with which to exorcise the endless abyss of female enjoyment, the mystery of the enjoyment of the Other and its ungovernable nature. How does a man enjoy? This is plain to see, and not just in the erection and the detumescence of the organ during and after intercourse. It is there and we can see it because the phallus constitutes the paradigm of an enjoyment that is necessarily represented by the organ. But how does a woman enjoy? What does the male know of the anarchy, the restlessness and the impossibility of governing the Other sex's enjoyment, their foreign language? It is this invisible presence, resistant to any colonization of female enjoyment, that brings about the misogynist recourse to insult ('they are all whores!'), in an attempt to tame what will not be tamed, to cut back to size that which appears to be structurally outsized. The men that offend women are those who fear them most. Misogynist violence would want to brand its mark on the body of women, it would like to define the identitarian margins of that lawless enjoyment. But this endeavour is always destined to fail miserably. The foreign nature of the language of women, which Adorno and Horkheimer by no means coincidentally compared to the anarchistic restlessness of the Jew,[43] refuses the phallic alphabet founded on the obtuse domain of having, of owning property.

Killing Them in Order to 'Love' Them

A chilling paradigm of the refusal to learn the foreign language of women (which is the language of love) can be found in the necrophiliac psychosis of Lester Ballard, the disturbing protagonist of Cormac McCarthy's *Child of God*.[44] He kills women as it is the only way in which he can have a relationship of any kind with them. A fugitive, a stranger in his own home, ostracized by everyone, the son of a dead father who killed himself, leaving him the sole inheritance of his eyes 'run out on stems like a crawfish' in a lifeless, hanging corpse, this man is the most desperate paradigm of loving illiteracy. What has he received in inheritance from the Other but a dead body, with its eyes wide open with horror?[45] He will go on to live like a stray dog, wandering the forests of the land that used to be his father's, without a home, with no one – an orphan, he will live in absolute abandonment. No one will ever answer his scream.

And when, one autumn afternoon, whilst walking through the uninhabited woods he finds the bodies of a young couple that had decided to kill themselves, after some hesitation he copulates wildly with the dead girl before dragging her to his shed and making her his partner. He will make her up, dress her with clothes he buys for her, and possess her sexually again. Only dead things inhabit his life, as if his father's death continued to echo through his existence with all of its maleficent power.

When one bitterly cold night a fire destroys his squalid shed and burns the woman's corpse, Lester, torn apart by grief, begins to collect the corpses of other women. He becomes a serial killer. He kills young women in order to finally possess them, to have relations with them. Before death, the woman's body and her life generate nothing but anxiety in him. Only after having killed her does it become possible for him to establish an (entirely nonsensical) relationship with a woman, in the illusion of having made her silent forever. The body reduced to corpse should, in fact, allow for the definitive neutralization of anxiety. In reality, the victims must dramatically multiply, the corpses are accumulated in the unreachable refuge of uninhabited caves. But no murder will ever be able to silence the foreign language of woman. If Lester Ballard represents a kind of extreme paradigm of violence against women, it is because it is possible to catch sight in him of the nexus that unites the passage to the violent act with the anxiety of getting close to and encountering a woman in all its dramatic proof. In place of the encounter with the other sex and the difficult task of learning the foreign language of woman, violence is unleashed aiming to transform his innocent victims into dead objects.

The Joy of Forgiveness?

Love mixes the urge towards appropriation and the encounter with the freedom of the Other, the gift of oneself and the absolute exposure to the desire of the Other, with the sexual enjoyment of the Other's body. It is the desire to possess the Other and, at the same time, the desire for their fullest freedom. Appropriation and expropriation are called upon here in a unique movement that knows no synthesis. They are pushed to want to possess the Other, to enjoy their erotic body, but they are always already beyond any plan of reclusion, they are at the absolute exposure to the unknown of the Other's desire. Love moves between these two extremes – that of appropriation and that of absolute exposure – without ever finding a definite resolution between the two.

The first movement of love is not that of having, but that of conceding, of losing oneself, of absolute exposure, without reservation, to the Other. In this sense, the only condition of forgiveness is the recognition of the intractable and radically free nature of the Other's desire and its foreign language, of which the woman is the most radical incarnation. For this reason, the work of forgiveness reveals more than anything else how no design for appropriation of the Other will ever be able to guarantee the realization of love. The work of forgiveness, when it is successful, breaks the constitutive relationship between the I and the paranoid-narcissistic violence that drives it. It is a reversing, a withdrawal, most importantly a redesigning of one's own image. It is Jesus' gesture to the adulterous woman: to crouch down on the ground, collect oneself, transition from a purely punitive and vengeful version of the Law (that assigns guilt) to another, the Law of the word and of love. Forgiveness never gains its strength from the behaviour of the person who must receive it, from how, for example, the other can fix their error or prove themselves to have repented. It is only possible to forgive someone who has failed to keep their promise when considering the extent to which the subject who has been offended is capable of refounding a new 'Yes!', a new beginning. They can still want love to last forever, they can still recognize the other's 'immeasurable' value. This means traversing not so much the Other's guilt, but their lack. The work of forgiveness is first and foremost an extreme reckoning with one's own ideal image, to the point of understanding its real limit. The encounter with this limit, as also happens in the work of mourning, lightens, saves, removes the burden of guilt. It frees the subject from the spirit of revenge. There is a mysterious joy in forgiveness that lightens the lovers who know how to reach it. It carries with it the recognition of the Other as *heteros*, as a different life, a life far from any symbolic-narcissistic illusion, from any fusion between One and the Other. It carries with it the love for a real Other, non-ideal, not reduced to the reflection in a mirror that illuminates and enriches our I, but a unique existence that exists as pure exteriority. Oblative love as pure dedication to the Other, in pursuit of an impossible fusion, gives way to the perpetual oscillation that characterizes the work of forgiveness, between the experience of the fragmentation of my being – led back from the trauma of betrayal, beyond the improving function of the image – and the recognition of the inassimilable character of the one I love. As if the betrayal has caused that irrepressible margin of freedom to ring out, the freedom that the illusion of love would like as its prisoner but that is instead revealed to be absolute.

Forgiving Oneself

In the experience gathered by analysis, we frequently find many cases in which the greatest pain is felt by the one who has betrayed the promise, who has exposed a life together to the risk of destruction, more so even than the person who has been betrayed. One of my patients, for example, told me, distraught, of a brief affair with a man that she had 'enacted' simply to get her beloved husband's attention, which was fully absorbed by his career. Dramatically, this clandestine relationship had been discovered by the husband himself, who had then decided to forgive her, recognizing that he too was responsible for this 'enacting', having made his partner feel marginalized within his life. And yet this woman continued not to forgive herself for what she had done despite her husband's forgiveness. This was the reason why she entered into analysis. Very quickly it emerged that her difficulty in forgiving herself was not caused only by having lied and betrayed the trust of the person she loved most in the world. More profoundly, at play was her relationship with her own desire. What she could not bear was having betrayed herself, not having been up to her own, most authentic desire. Analysis would lead her to recognize that an urge to destroy what made her happy had prematurely been a part of her childhood, dominated by a mother too wounded by life to transmit a positive sense of desire to her daughter. As a child when she felt particularly full of life and happiness she would be struck by a kind of fit that would lead her to destroy all of her favourite toys. In doing so she attempted to satisfy a voracious and inflexible maternal Super-Ego. A recent scene in her life would always come to mind: not long before entering the tunnel of her brief affair, during a drink with friends who were moaning in sterile fashion about their love lives, she had thought to herself: 'I pray that all of this happiness that I am enjoying with my husband and my family never ends!' In the next few weeks her mother was diagnosed with a very serious illness. This young woman's happiness was once more prohibited by the maternal shadow. In a dream, as she was playing in a field next to her parents' house as she had done as a child, she sees the terrifying image of a black cow's wide-open mouth emerging from the grass, trying to grab her and drag her down into the bowels of the earth. She immediately associates this image with her mother's unsatisfied life and the black of the animal's coat with the dark sadness that had always made her stand out. When she learnt of her mother's illness she unconsciously had to demolish her love and her family, betraying her desire, endangering her whole life, throwing everything away as she had done with her toys as a child, in an attempt to escape from the grip of the maternal Super-Ego. But as would also happen when she was a child, rather than help free her, this only served to consolidate the grasp of this ferocious Super-Ego, making real the absolute and distressed subordination to an Other who did not allow her to live her own happiness. The analysis led her to recognize in the act of betrayal this obedience to the maternal will that had been interiorized as an oppressive voice. 'Life is a horror, happiness does not exist!', her mother would repeat to her from the moment she was born. Before being worthy of the Other's forgiveness she had to forgive herself not so much for having betrayed her husband, but for betraying her own most profound desire: her right to separate herself from her mother, to desire, her right to find her own measure of happiness, her vow to be satisfied by love beyond the maternal unhappiness.

Notes

Introduction

1 See Sigmund Freud, 'Contributions to the Psychology of Love', in *The Standard Edition of the Complete Psychological Works of Sigmund Freud. Vol. XI (1910): Five Lectures on Psycho-Analysis, Leonardo da Vinci and Other Works*, Vintage, London 2001, pp. 163–90.

2 Paul Éluard, 'Le dur désir du durer' ['The Firm Desire to Endure'], in *Last Love Poetry*, Black Widow Press, Boston 2006.

3 See Freud, 'Contributions to the Psychology of Love'.

4 'Only love allows enjoyment to condescend to desire' (Jacques Lacan, *The Seminar of Jacques Lacan. Book X: Anxiety*, Polity, Cambridge 2014, p. 179).

Chapter 1 The Ideology of the New

1 T. W. Adorno, *Minima moralia: Reflections on an Offended Life*, Verso, London 2005, pp. 181–2.

2 See Freud, 'Contributions to the Psychology of Love'. A highly informative Lacanian reading of Freud's text can be

found in Jacques-Alain Miller, *Logiche della vita amorosa* [*Logic of a Love Life*], ed. A. Di Ciaccia, Astrolabio, Rome 1997, pp. 11–57.

3 On this new and specific degradation of love, see the particularly accurate observations made by Charles Melman in *L'uomo senza gravità: Conversazioni con Jean-Pierre Lebrun* [*Man Without Gravity: Conversations with Jean-Pierre Lebrun*], trans. Bruno Mondadori, Milan 2011, pp. 32–4. For the French original, see *L'homme sans gravité*, Gallimard, Paris 2005.

4 An intense and ironic depiction of this dilemma can be found in Antonio Scurati's novel *Il padre infedele* [*The Unfaithful Father*], Bompiani, Milan 2013.

5 Robin Dunbar, *The Science of Love*, Faber and Faber, London 2012, p. 50.

6 Dunbar, *Science of Love*, pp. 34–42.

7 Lacanian psychoanalyst Darian Leader goes even further in this direction with cutting irony: 'a man who vows eternal love or demands eternal fidelity is also likely to talk silly', in *Promises Lovers Make When It Gets Late*, Faber and Faber, London 1998, p. 10.

8 This is the thesis that Freud broadly develops in 'Instincts and Their Vicissitudes', demonstrating how in the build-up of instincts the only thing that really counts for the drive is its own satisfaction. The object, therefore, appears only as a means through which the drive is satisfied, as '[that which] is most variable about an instinct', Freud writes. See Sigmund Freud, *The Standard Edition of the Complete Psychological Works of Sigmund Freud. Vol. XIV (1914–1916): On the History of the Psycho-Analytic*

Movement, Papers on Metapsychology and Other Works, Vintage, London 2001, pp. 109–40, in particular p. 122.

9 The two main texts in which Freud theorizes love as logical blindness and an infatuated and narcissistic idealization of the self through the beloved object elevated to the ideal Ego are 'On Narcissism: An Introduction' and 'Group Psychology and the Analysis of the Ego' in, respectively: Freud, *Standard Edition*, vol. XIV, pp. 73–104, and *The Standard Edition of the Complete Psychological Works of Sigmund Freud. Vol. XVIII (1920–1922): Beyond the Pleasure Principle, Group Psychology and Other Works*, Vintage, London 2001, pp. 68–144.

10 This anthropological mutation is at the centre of my work *L'uomo senza inconscio: Figure della nuova clinica psicoanalitica* [*Man Without Unconscious: Figures in New Psychoanalytic Treatment*], Raffaello Cortina, Milan 2010.

11 See Massimo Recalcati, *Clinica del vuoto: Anoressie, dipendenze e psicosi* [*Treating the Void: Anorexia, Addiction, Psychosis*], Franco Angeli, Milan 2002.

12 Max Weber, 'The Protestant Ethic and the Spirit of Capitalism', in *The Protestant Ethic and the Spirit of Capitalism, and Other Writings*, Penguin, London 2002, pp. 1–200.

13 See Jacques Lacan, 'Della psicoanalisi nei suoi rapporti con la realtà' ['On Psychoanalysis and Its Relation with Reality'], in *Altri scritti* [*Other Writings*], ed. A. Di Ciaccia, Einaudi, Turin 2013, p. 351. For the original, see *De la psychanalyse dans ses rapports avec la réalité*, in *Autres écrits*, Seuil, Paris 2001.

14 Zygmunt Bauman, *Liquid Love: On the Frailty of Human Bonds*, Polity, Cambridge 2003.

15 This is a thesis developed with courage and poetry in a recent text by the materialist philosopher Alain Badiou, who speaks (in a Christian sense) of love as 'eternity descending into time', in *In Praise of Love*, Serpent's Tail, London 2012, p. 47.

16 Martin Heidegger, 'The Origin of the Work of Art', in *Basic Writings*, Routledge, London 2010, pp. 83–140.

17 Heidegger, 'Origin of the Work of Art'.

18 The reference to the portulaca is an homage to Michele Serra, *Gli sdraiati*, Feltrinelli, Milan 2013.

19 See F. Scarabicchi, *L'esperienza della neve* [*The Experience of Snow*], Donzelli, Rome 2003.

20 Jacques Lacan, *The Seminar of Jacques Lacan. Book XX: On Feminine Sexuality, The Limits of Love and Knowledge: Encore*, W. W. Norton, London 1999.

21 See Saint Augustine, *Confessions*, Penguin, London 1961, pp. 164–5.

22 Shakespeare, *Romeo and Juliet*, Act 2, Scene 2, 140–1.

Chapter 2 Encounter and Destiny

1 Ludwig Feuerbach, *The Essence of Christianity*, Dover, Mineola 2008.

2 All of these themes are developed in particular in Freud, 'On Narcissism'.

3 Pier Paolo Pasolini, *Scritti Corsari* [*Corsair Writings*], Garzanti, Milan 1990.

4 Jacques Lacan, 'The Mirror Stage as Formative of the *I* Function', in *Écrits*, trans. Bruce Fink, W. W. Norton, New York 2006. See, in particular, p. 78.

5 See Lacan, *Seminar of Jacques Lacan. Book X*, p. 313.

6 Genesis 22.

7 Arthur Schopenhauer, *The World as Will and Representation*, Cambridge University Press, Cambridge 2010.

8 The Freudian figure of the *Nebenmensch* is central to the dialectic of desire as reconstructed by Freud in 'Project for a Scientific Psychology', in *The Standard Edition of the Complete Psychological Works of Sigmund Freud. Vol. I (1886–1899): Pre-Psycho Analytic Publications and Unfinished Drafts*, Vintage, London 2001, pp. 283–346.

9 Jesus' scream condenses within it the essence of Christianity as exposed to the experience of absolute abandonment. 'His death – that of Christ – was not, like the death of Socrates resigned and impassive, but the death of the *man who screams*. That scream is asking God to be close to us [. . .] Our God is a God who has pathos within him, a God who suffers out of love. Our God is the God who suffers, the God who, in Jesus, accepted not only pain and death, but even the infamy of one who dies on the cross, damned by God and rejected by men' (Enzo Bianchi, *I paradossi della croce* [*The Paradoxes of the Cross*], Morcelliana, Brescia 2006, pp. 35–9 [author's italics]). The emphasis on the scream and abandonment in Christ's experience also occupies a central position in the important theological reflection by P. Coda, *Il logos e il nulla: Trinità, religioni, mistica* [*The Logos and the Void: Trinity, Religion, Mysticism*], Città Nuova, Rome 2004, in particular pp. 206–25.

10 'To you LORD I call; you are my rock, do not turn a deaf ear to me. For if you remain silent I will be like those who go down to the pit' (Psalm 28:1).

11 This is a sentiment repeated throughout Lacan's work. For reference, see Jacques Lacan, *The Seminar of Jacques Lacan. Book V: Formations of the Unconscious*, Polity, Cambridge 2017, p. 194.

12 The gift of love in the parent–child relationship does not end with the translation of the scream into the demand for love, in the response 'Here I am!' to the child's cries. In *The Telemachus Complex* I insist on the equally central importance of a second gift, made possible by the first. After having responded to the scream, having taken care of the life that is entrusted to them, the parents' love must also know how to let this life go, to be able to lose it, abandon it. At play here is the gift of freedom. Allowing life to go where its desire lies. This implies being able to give one's own insufficiency. Not to demand always having the last word on the meaning of life and death, but allowing the child to experience the freedom of the desert. As a result, the parents' love becomes 'ill' when it manifests itself as pure abandonment or as a pure urge for cannibalistic absorption. See Massimo Recalcati, *The Telemachus Complex*: *Parents and Children After the Decline of the Father*, Polity, Cambridge 2019.

13 Lacan, *Seminar of Jacques Lacan. Book XX*.

14 This is only discovered by the young protagonist of *Into the Wild* (dir. Sean Penn, 2017) at the end of his solitary journey through the United States and Northern Mexico to the inhospitable and majestic territories of Alaska, where he meets his death: 'Happiness is only real when shared.'

15 Jacques Lacan, *Seminar of Jacques Lacan. Book X*, p. 337.

16 Jean-Luc Nancy, *Sull'amore* [*On Love*], Bollati Boringhieri, Turin 2009, pp. 33 and 35. For the French original see Nancy, *'Je*

t'aime, un peu, beaucoup, passionnément' [*'I love you, a bit, a lot, passionately'*], Bayard, Paris 2008.

17 'One wants to be loved for everything – not only for one's ego, as Descartes says, but for the colour of one's hair, for one's idiosyncrasies, for one's weaknesses, for everything'. (Jacques Lacan, *The Seminar of Jacques Lacan. Book I: Freud's Papers on Techniques 1953–1954*, W. W. Norton, London 1991, p. 276).

18 Badiou, *In Praise of Love*, p. 26.

19 Jean-Paul Sartre, *Being and Nothingness: An Essay in Phenomenological Ontology*, Routledge, Abingdon 2018.

20 Sartre, *Being and Nothingness*, p. 491.

21 Lacan, *Seminar of Jacques Lacan. Book XX*.

22 Freud, 'On Narcissism'.

23 Lacan, *Seminar of Jacques Lacan. Book X*.

24 Nancy, *Sull'amore*, p. 33.

25 This leads, among other things, to a revision of Lacan's thesis according to which sexual enjoyment is always and only enjoyment of one's own (phallic) organ and each of the Two remains in the impossibility of accessing the enjoyment of the Other. The loving experience, on the other hand, demonstrates how the Other's enjoyment increases the enjoyment of the One and, as such, is in no way insensitive to this. This is the general direction of a number of lucid observations contained in G. Pommier, *Que veut dire 'faire' l'amour?* [*What Does It Mean To 'Make' Love?*], Flammarion, Paris 2010.

26 From this perspective, the impossibility of reconciling 'passionate love' and 'love as a gift of oneself' lies in the field of neuroses even if it reveals something that touches the structure of loving

desire: sexual desire pushes the object and its enjoyment, whilst love for the subject pushes towards the subject and its desire. Nevertheless, we know that the power of love lies in strengthening and not diluting the function of the object that causes desire. This is how I translate Lacan's indication that only love can cause desire to converge with enjoyment. When Nancy talks about the impossibility of reconciling desire and abandonment, sex and Other, between a love that is made and one that is received, between the Christian version of love as a gift of oneself and the Greek version of love as erotic passion, it ends up, unfortunately, once again putting forward the Freudian thesis that the disjuncture between love and desire is insurmountable. Although it does rather contradictorily remind us that without the convergence of these two versions of love – the Christian and the Greek – this disjuncture would sterilely resolve itself in the 'frenzy of desire' or in the 'exaltation of faith that is equally sterile if uncoupled from the eros of the body' (Nancy, *Sull'amore*, in particular pp. 47–9).

27 This also stands for the encounter with God, given the way in which the great mystics speak. It is a thesis we find in Lacan. See *Seminar of Jacques Lacan. Book XX*, pp. 64–77.

28 Men tend to overlook the effective value of fidelity. They are too quick to distinguish the fidelity of the heart and that of the body. Conversely, women tend to be unfaithful when there is no love in the heart or when that love has been disappointed. The male parallelism that separates fidelity of the body from that of the heart appears foreign to women. Men, however, do not understand how the body can remain faithful over time, but then

react furiously to the physical infidelity of their partner. This is why Freud, whilst locating the unconscious basis for female jealousy in the anxiety of losing the object of their love, maintained that masculine jealousy was eminently projective: a particularly jealous male is the one who is particularly unfaithful.

29 See Enzo Bianchi, 'Il dono e il perdono' ['The Gift and Forgiveness'], conference held at Bose, 10 March 2013.

30 See Saint Augustine, *Confessions*.

Chapter 3   Trauma and Abandonment

1 All of these themes are present in Lacan, *Seminar of Jacques Lacan. Book XX*. For a more in-depth analysis, see my book *Jacques Lacan: Desiderio, godimento e soggettivazione* [*Jacques Lacan: Desire, Enjoyment and Subjectivization*], Raffaello Cortina, Milan 2013, ch. 5.

2 Sartre, *Being and Nothingness*, p. 486.

3 Marcel Proust, *In Search of Lost Time. Vol. 5: The Captive*, Modern Library, New York 1982, pp. 75–6.

4 Proust, *In Search of Lost Time*, vol. 5, pp. 313–14.

5 'I am searching the other's body as if I wanted to see what was inside it, as if the mechanical cause of my desire were in the adverse body (I am like those children who take a clock apart to find out what time is)' (Roland Barthes, *A Lover's Discourse: Fragments*, Penguin, London 1979, p. 71).

6 Proust, *In Search of Lost Time*, vol. 5, p. 82.

7 Jacques Lacan, *The Seminar of Jacques Lacan. Book VI: Desire and Its Interpretations*, Polity, Cambridge 2019.

8　See Jacques Derrida, *Lo spergiuro* [*The Deceit*], Castelvecchi, Vicenza 2013,

9　This is what Jacques Derrida defines as the 'two-pronged structure' of every vow: 'I have sincerely promised in the past, but time has indeed passed, passed or surpassed, and whoever has made a promise, be it recently or long ago, can remain faithful to their promise, but I am no longer me, I am no longer the same me, I am another, *I* is an other, I have changed, everything has changed, even those to whom the promise was made. I have forgotten [. . .]. For example: I had fallen in love, I am no longer in love in the same way, I love someone else, and I am incapable of realising, I, ask the other who in me is deciding this in my place.' It is in this sense, Derrida says, that 'someone is already lying, already perjuring themselves in the moment they take that vow and promise' (Derrida, *Lo spergiuro*, pp. 30–1).

10　Jacques Lacan, *The Seminar of Jacques Lacan. Book III: The Psychoses 1959–1966*, W. W. Norton, London 1997.

11　The Freudian thesis that relates the trauma of childhood seduction and rape to the realization of an unconscious desire that is inadmissible to the conscience and present in the subject ('If what they [the subjects] long for the most intensely in their phantasies is presented to them in reality, they none the less flee from it' (Sigmund Freud, 'Fragments of an Analysis of a Case of Hysteria', in *The Standard Edition of the Complete Psychological Works of Sigmund Freud. Vol. VII (1901–1905): A Case of Hysteria, Three Essays on Sexuality and Other Works*, Vintage, London 2001, p. 110)) should be balanced out with this other version of trauma that exposes the subject to the collapse of the Other.

12 Jean Améry, *At the Mind's Limits: Contemplations by a Survivor on Auschwitz and its Realities*, Indiana University Press, Bloomington 1980, pp. 27–8. I owe my knowledge of this passage to Mario Rossi Monti (University of Urbino).

13 On the theme of trust in the Other that is necessary for human life, see Enzo Bianchi, *Fede e fiducia* [*Faith and Trust*], Einaudi, Turin 2013.

14 Jacques Lacan, *The Seminar of Jacques Lacan. Book XI: The Four Fundamental Concepts of Psychoanalysis*, W. W. Norton, London 1998.

15 This absence of rest, this impossibility of separating oneself from the object, lies at the heart of the figure of the 'one despairing in love' described in singular tones by Stefano Bonaga in *Sulla disperazione d'amore* [*On Despair in Love*], Aliberti, Rome 2011.

16 See Lacan, *Seminar of Jacques Lacan. Book X.*

17 See Derrida, *Lo spergiuro.*

Chapter 4 The Work of Forgiveness

1 See Sigmund Freud, 'Civilization and Its Discontents', in *The Standard Edition of the Complete Psychological Works of Sigmund Freud. Vol. XXI (1927–1931): The Future of An Illusion, Civilization and Its Discontents and Other Works*, Vintage, London 2001, pp. 64–148.

2 Lacan, 'Aggressiveness in Psychoanalysis', in *Écrits*, pp. 82–101.

3 'Of course, true love is the exception – roughly two or three instances in a century' (Albert Camus, *The Fall*, Penguin, London 2006, p. 360.

4 'For romantic pairings as much as friendships, there is an inevitable deterioration over time [. . .]. However, unlike pet dogs (whose devotion seems to be unqualified), we seem to have an innate tendency to trade on our relationships, sometimes pushing them to their limit to gain advantage for ourselves. Pushed too far, even the most devoted relationship can reach the point of exasperation and collapse' (Dunbar, *Science of Love*, p. 126).

5 The Law of the Old Testament does not concede any forgiveness to the sin of adultery, for either men or women: 'If a man commits adultery with another man's wife – with the wife of his neighbour – both the adulterer and the adulteress are to be put to death' (Leviticus 20:10). 'If a man is found sleeping with another man's wife, both the man who slept with her and the woman must die' (Deuteronomy 22:22).

6 Françoise Dolto, *I vangeli alla luce della psicoanalisi: La liberazione del desiderio* [*The Gospels in Light of Psychoanalysis: The Liberation of Desire*], et al., Milan 2012, p. 171. Her wide-reaching study of adultery is developed on pp. 167–86.

7 See Bianchi, *Paradossi della croce*, p. 107. In Saint Paul we can clearly find the two steps on which Jesus founds the possibility of the gesture of forgiveness. The first calls for the suspension of the automatic and impersonal application of the Law of Moses ('Christ is the culmination of the Law' (Romans 10:4)), while the second calls for the introduction of another Law, that of love and forgiveness, which entirely exceeds the first disciplinary and super-egoic version of the Law itself ('Love is the fulfilment of the Law' (Romans 10:4)). On this theme I would recommend the

extraordinary work by Alain Badiou, *Saint Paul: The Foundation of Universalism*, Stanford University Press, Stanford 2003.

8 Lacan, 'Kant with Sade', in *Écrits*, pp. 645–70.

9 Jacques Derrida, *On Cosmopolitanism and Forgiveness*, Routledge, London 1997, p. 32.

10 Lacan, *Seminar of Jacques Lacan. Book I.*

11 Lacan, *Seminar of Jacques Lacan. Book I*, p. 276.

12 See Bianchi, 'Dono e perdono'. The reference to the words of Jesus, 'Do not let your left hand know what your right hand is doing', captures, according to Bianchi, the entirely asymmetrical posture of forgiveness. In this sense, the essence of Christianity would be the entirely free experience of love. For more on these themes, see Paul Ricoeur, *Memory, History, Forgetting*, University of Chicago Press, Chicago 2006.

13 Freud, 'Fragment of an Analysis of a Case of Hysteria', in *Standard Edition*, vol. VII, p. 43.

14 Freud, 'Mourning and Melancholia', in *Standard Edition*, vol. XIV, pp. 243–58.

15 Freud, 'Mourning and Melancholia'.

16 'Each death declares each time the end of the world in totality, the end of every world, and each time the end of the world as unique totality, thus irreplaceable and thus infinite' (Jacques Derrida, *Ogni volta unica, la fine del mondo* [*Each Time Unique, the End of the World*], Jaca Book, Milan 2005, p. 11). Each time we mourn, the person who is not there takes away a world, 'a world that is for us the whole world, the only world, which sinks into an abyss from which no memory – even if we keep the memory, and we will keep it – can save it' (Jacques Derrida, *The*

Work of Mourning, University of Chicago Press, Chicago 2001 p.115). See also the introduction by P. A. Brault and M. Naas, 'Fare i conti con i morti: Jacques Derrida e la politica del lutto' ['Reckoning with the Dead: Jacques Derrida and the Politics of Mourning'], and the observations made by L. Barani in the volume on Derrida, *Derrida e il dono del lutto* [*Derrida and the Gift of Mourning*], Anterem Edizioni, Verona 2009.

17 C. S. Lewis, *A Grief Observed*, HarperCollins, New York 1996, p. 8.

18 Jacques Derrida, *The Politics of Friendship*, Verso, London 2005.

19 Lewis, *Grief Observed*, p. 11.

20 Freud, 'Mourning and Melancholia'.

21 'In real mourning, it is the "test of reality" which shows me that the loved object has ceased to exist. In amorous mourning, the object is neither dead nor remote. It is I who decide that its image must die [. . .] As long as this strange mourning lasts, I will therefore have to undergo two contrary miseries: to suffer from the fact that the other is present (continuing, in spite of himself, to wound me) and to suffer from the fact that the other is dead (dead at least as I loved him)' (Roland Barthes, *Lover's Discourse*, pp. 106–7).

22 Lacan, 'Mirror Stage', pp. 75–81.

23 Melanie Klein, *Envy and Gratitude and Other Works 1946–1963*, Vintage, London 1997.

24 See S. Thanopulos, 'Winnicott e la separazione' ['Winnicott and Separation'], in S. Pozzoli, ed., *Il concetto di separazione nella teoria e nella pratica psicoanalitica* [*The Concept of Separation in Psychoanalytic Theory and Practice*], Poiesis, Bari 2010, pp. 61–79.

25 Lacan, *Seminar of Jacques Lacan. Book XX*.

26 Lacan, 'A Theoretical Introduction to the Functions of Psychoanalysis in Criminology', in *Écrits*, pp. 102–22, particularly p. 120.

27 Freud, 'Mourning and Melancholia', p. 253.

28 In a positive sense, it can be used in eroticism as a stimulant for desire that in no way excludes a particular 'good' use of violence, as is well demonstrated by G. Pommier in *Del buon uso erotico della collera e di qualche sua conseguenza* [*On the Good Erotic Use of Anger, and Some of Its Consequences*], Raffaello Cortina, Milan 2013. In an entirely negative sense, it takes the form of the man's predatory subjugation of the Other sex that destroys desire and sexuality itself.

29 For an excellent overview of these themes I refer you to a conference held by Claudia Rubini, a young psychoanalyst from Bologna, who clearly synthesizes the problem of the relationship between violence and repetition in the female universe much more effectively than other authors, who perhaps carry a little too much baggage. See Claudia Rubini, 'Prima che sia tardi: Incontro con la violenza' ['Before It Is Too Late: Encounter with Violence'], in *Letter(a)*, 4, 2014.

30 At the great turning point of the 1920s, Freud theorized the death drive (*Todestrieb*) as the force that pushes the human towards an excess of enjoyment that does not consider the protection of life but that instead leads life towards ruin. See Freud, 'Beyond the Pleasure Principle', in *Standard Edition*, vol. XVIII, pp. 7–66.

31 We must highlight in this case, as in many others, the high incidence of maternal depression. It is often the afflicted and defeated

destiny of mothers to not transmit anything to their daughters except the mortifying need to passively adapt to the male fantasy. This is the theme of Lucrezio Lerro's novel set in an isolated town in the deepest Italian South, in which we find the portrait of mothers crushed by the arrogance and ignorance of *machismo*. Women who, instead of rebelling against it, make it their own, flattening themselves onto that fantasy that humiliates them most. In this case it is the acquiescence shown by these mothers that does not allow for the transmission of desire from one generation to another. It appears as one great, spectral miscarriage: shrivelled life transmits only death without life. How is it possible in these cases for a daughter not to replicate the maternal unhappiness? Not to let herself be contaminated by apathy and the maternal tendency to self-flagellation? Not think that the only thing that counts in a woman, as these mothers seem to believe and transmit to their daughters, that the only thing that counts as a woman is 'getting yourself married' at any cost? See Lucrezia Lerro, *La confraternita delle puttane* [*The Confraternity of Whores*], Mondadori, Milan 2013.

32 See Massimo Recalcati, *Ritratti del desiderio* [*Portraits of Desire*], Raffaello Cortina, Milan 2012.

33 Jealousy as a work of thought, as an incessant imaginary lucubration, is a trait of human love lives. There is no equivalent in the animal kingdom despite what some neuroscientists may think, noting, for example, how 'Hamadryas baboons are so jealous that should one of their females so much as allow another male to get between them, even completely by accident, the male will launch a savage attack on her, with vicious bites to the nape of

the neck' (Dunbar, *Science of Love*, p. 121). Human jealousy is not unleashed when faced with the reality of a betrayal that has taken place, but when faced with details (think of Desdemona's handkerchief in Shakespeare's tragedy *Othello*), doubts, minor uncertainties and ambiguities. It is an elaboration, sometimes close to delirium, provoked by the anxiety of losing the object of one's own love because of the intrusion of an Other, without there necessarily being any proof of their actual presence. It is an entirely psychological fact that may have no bearing whatsoever on the real existence of the Other. This is why it is possible to be jealous of the dead or of the past of the ones we desire. In this sense, as Proust shows us, 'jealousy is thus endless, for even if the beloved, by dying for instance, can no longer provoke it by her actions, it may happen that memories subsequent to any event suddenly materialise and behave in our minds as if they too were events, memories, which hitherto we had never explored [. . .] There is no need for there to be two of you, it is enough to be alone in your room, thinking of fresh betrayals by your mistress to come to light, even though she is dead' (Proust, *In Search of Lost Time*, vol. 5, pp. 72–3).

34 See Plato, *The Symposium*, Penguin, London 1999.

35 Medea, on the other hand, is the female example invoked by Lacan to demonstrate the crazed, limitless dimension of female love. It is her love for Jason that causes Medea to react to his betrayal by killing all of her children, tragically demonstrating how maternal love can never satisfy a woman's (infinite) demand for love.

36 This is a recurrent theme in the novels of Philip Roth when it

comes to the difficulty of relationships between generations. Among the best examples we find Lucy Nelson, the protagonist of *When She Was Good*, Penguin, London 2007.

37 See Recalcati, *L'uomo senza inconscio*.

38 Jacques Lacan, *Television: A Challenge to the Psychoanalytic Establishment*, W. W. Norton, London 1990, p. 22.

39 See Jacques Lacan, *The Seminar of Jacques Lacan. Book VII: The Ethics of Psychoanalysis (1959–1960)*, W. W. Norton, London 1997, p. 237.

40 Sigmund Freud, 'Analysis Terminable and Interminable', in *The Standard Edition of the Complete Psychological Works of Sigmund Freud. Vol. XXIII (1937–1939): Moses and Monotheism, An Outline of Psychoanalysis and Other Works*, Vintage, London 2001, pp. 216–54, particularly pp. 250–2.

41 See Lacan, 'Lo stordito' ['The Blunderer'], in *Altri scritti*, p. 464. For the original, see 'L'étourdit', in *Autres écrits*.

42 In the case of a young anorexic woman, the petrification of the body was a response to the brutality of male enjoyment. Amelia lived her anorexia as a sort of emotional anaesthesia: she defined it as literally 'being turned to marble'. This same expression emerged in the chain of free associations during a session in which she was remembering a scene from her childhood. In it, she heard her drunken father in her parents' room, which was situated next to her own, violently force himself on her mother. She heard it all and had to cancel it out. Her ears would close up, her body would go stiff, her blood would freeze, whilst she 'turned to marble'.

43 T. W. Adorno and M. Horkheimer, *Dialectic of Enlightenment*, Verso, London 1997.

44 Cormac McCarthy, *Child of God*, Picador, London 2010.

45 It is interesting to compare *Child of God* with McCarthy's *The Road* (Picador, London 2006), with the latter the response to the psychotic universe of *Child of God*, or, if you prefer, with *Child of God* depicting the son's destiny when deprived of the presence of paternal testimony found in *The Road*. Whilst in *The Road* a father protects his son's life, his breath, he decides not to commit suicide but to resist in a Godless world devastated by the blind law of violence, in *Child of God* the father chooses suicide, he resigns from his symbolic function, leaving his own son in absolute abandonment, he abandons him to his own scream. For a reading of *The Road* by McCarthy, I would recommend my book *Cosa resta del padre? La paternità nell'epoca ipermoderna* [*What Remains of the Father? Fatherhood in the Hypermodern Era*], Raffaello Cortina, Milan 2011, pp. 155–69.